GEARHEAD MANIA

SUPERCARS
DRIVING THE DREAM

ADAM PHILLIPS

ROSEN
PUBLISHING®
New York

This edition published in 2013 by:

The Rosen Publishing Group, Inc.
29 East 21st Street
New York, NY 10010

Library of Congress Cataloging-in-Publication Data

Phillips, Adam.
Supercars: driving the dream/Adam Phillips.—1st ed.
   p. cm.—(Gearhead mania)
Includes bibliographical references and index.
ISBN 978-1-4488-9213-6 (library binding)
1. Sports cars—History. 2. Sports cars—Pictorial works. 3. Automobiles, Racing—History. I. Title. II. Series: Gearhead mania.
TL236.P485 2013
629.222—dc23

2012032055

Manufactured in the United States of America

CPSIA Compliance Information: Batch #W12YA: For further information, contact Rosen Publishing, New York, New York, at 1-800-237-9932.

Under license from Igloo Books Ltd.
Cottage Farm, Mears Ashby Road,
Sywell, Northants, NN6 0BJ, England
Copyright © 2012 Igloo Books Ltd.

Contents

What makes someone want to buy a car that costs a small fortune? Or a very large one for that matter? Surely a nice little Japanese hatchback with a 1.4-liter engine will do the job. After all, you don't need 1,000 bhp to pop down to the local shopping center or to pick up the kids from school. But that's missing the point – we humans have a passion for pushing forward; for wanting to outdo and challenge ourselves, and supercars are one of the ultimate expressions of this desire. And people will always want to buy into that.

Naturally, there are those who merely want a supercar as a trophy, to be driven once in a while to impress their friends. Equally, there are those who understand that only the best will do, who want to experience the sensation and thrill of cars designed for pure driver indulgence. And if we can't afford them, then we want to respect and admire the creativity and engineering that has made the supercar what it is today.

After all, the early days of supercar development were exciting ones – bold but small steps into the future where one supercar would offer the greatest performance while the other would deliver the best driving experience. And now the fruits of all that blood, sweat and tears over the past five decades are seemingly reaching their peak. From Britain and Italy through to America and Japan, the combined genius of designers and engineers has seen the supercars of today blend so many elements perfectly.

And they have to – we're a demanding bunch after all. We want those looks – the ones that linger in the mind well after glimpsing that exotic machinery for the first time. We want to know about the performance – the kind that defies belief when first scanning down a supercar's specifications. And we want the handling – the kind that offers huge grip, accessibility and feedback. Yes, we're a demanding bunch.

Modern supercars offer the best of all worlds (well, apart from the miles-per-gallon and luggage space that is) – and this book is a tribute to them. From supercars on a budget to exotica that can cost you a fortune, the automotive art featured in these pages show that we're all still as passionate about progress, and going fast, as we ever were.

The only question remaining is – if this is as good as it gets now, just what will be rolling down our roads in the future? We can't wait. Can you?

The History of the Supercar

There has never been a better time than now for supercar aficionados to indulge in their passion for automobile excellence. However, it has taken over 50 years of cumulative development and hard work by the world's greatest designers and engineers to bring us up to the modern day. Here we present some of the highlights of the supercar's emergence since its birth in the 1950s.

1950s

Mercedes 300SL Gullwing (1954-1957)

This is not a true supercar, but it is one that showed the way forward because of its incredible technology and performance; the 3-liter engine, producing 240 bhp, could make the sprint from 0-60 in 8.8 secs and hit a top speed of 145 mph (233 km/h).

Innovations in technology saw the 300SL become the first ever production car to have fuel injection, and the car featured a space-frame chassis which, because of the chassis running down either side of the car, meant the 300SL had to have those now-famous gullwing doors.

Specifications

ENGINE	2996 cc
MAX POWER	240 bhp at 6,100 rpm
MAX TORQUE	217 lb ft at 4,800 rpm
0-60 MPH (0–100 KM/H)	8.8 secs
TOP SPEED	135 mph+ (217 km/h)

Copyright Ford Motor Company Ltd

Ford GT40 MkIII
(1967)

Ford's race car version of the GT40 humiliated Ferrari at Le Mans in the latter half of the 1960s (see page 60). It also spawned a street version in 1967 that was panned by critics for its sloppy handling. But serious drivers didn't care about that because the GT40 MkIII could outrun its competitors in a straight line with the 306 bhp produced by its 4.7-liter V8 engine 0-60 mph (100 km/h) acceleration in 5.5 secs. Its top speed of 170 mph (234 km/h) also hinted at what the future held for true supercars. Only seven GT40s (MkIII) were ever built.

Specifications

ENGINE	4736 cc
MAX POWER	306 bhp at 6,000 rpm
MAX TORQUE	229 lb ft at 4,200 rpm
0-60 MPH (0–100 KM/H)	5.5 secs
TOP SPEED	170 mph (274 km/h)

Copyright Ford Motor Company Ltd

Lamborghini Muira
(1966–1972)

Unveiled in 1966, the Muira is what many believe to be the planet's first true supercar, partly because its mid-mounted engine was a first. The greatest version of Muira is the SV produced at the beginning of the 1970s, which saw the original's 350 bhp increased to 385 bhp. The only problem

Lamborghini Muira SV specifications (1974-1982)

ENGINE	3929 cc
MAX POWER	385 bhp at 7,850 rpm
MAX TORQUE	294 lb ft at 5,750 rpm
0-60 MPH (0–100 KM/H)	6.0 secs
TOP SPEED	180 mph (290 km/h)

with the Muira is that the front end is prone to lift at high speeds.

Other key cars from the 1960s: Jaguar E-Type, Ferrari 365 GTB Daytona, Corvette Sting Ray, De Tomaso Mangus

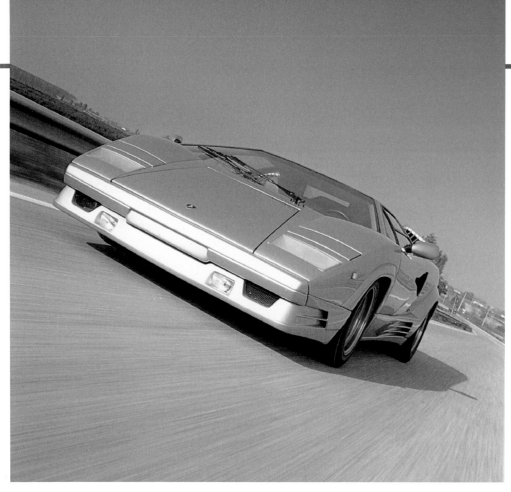

Lamborghini Countach 25th Anniversary (1989–1990)

Lamborghini Countach (1974–1990)

It's one of the iconic styles in car history – the prototype Countach, which was shown for the first time in 1971, was greeted with great fanfare by the crowds. The replacement for the Muira, the sleek, sensual lines had been supplanted with dramatic lines and a wedge shape that would come to dominate the supercar world for the next ten years. The first Lamborghini Countach to be released (the LP400) featured a 3.9-liter V12 engine that could make the sprint from 0-60 mph (0-100 km/h) in 5.6 secs. Several incarnations of the Countach, which included the celebrated 5-liter Countach QV in 1985, followed over its illustrious 17-year reign as the king of the supercars. It has to be said though that the Countach represents the ultimate old-school supercar – it offered a driving experience that had to be learned; simply getting behind the wheel and flooring it was not to be recommended.

LP400 specifications (1974-1982)

ENGINE	3929 cc
MAX POWER	375 bhp at 8,000 rpm
MAX TORQUE	268 lb ft at 5,000 rpm
0-60 MPH (0-100 KM/H)	5.6 secs
TOP SPEED	180 mph+ (290 km/h)

BMW M1
(1978–1981)

The M1 is one of the unsung heroes of the 1970s. It was BMW's first (and, so far, only) foray into creating a mid-engined supercar, and it could have worked out if the project hadn't been besieged by problems. It was intended that the M1 would be styled and built by Lamborghini, but because the raging bull was experiencing money woes, Bauer, in Germany, produced the car for BMW. The car had been intended for the track but these plans fell through. It's a tragedy because the road-going M1 beat its Italian rivals by offering the same levels of grip but pairing it with forgiving handling and great reliability.

Specifications

ENGINE	3453 cc
MAX POWER	277 bhp at 6,500 rpm
MAX TORQUE	243 lb ft at 5,000 rpm
0-60 MPH (0-100 KM/H)	5.6 secs
TOP SPEED	162 mph (261 km/h)

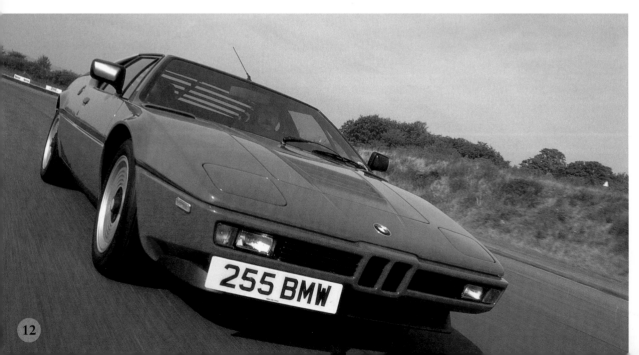

Other key cars from the 1970s: Maserati Bora, Porsche 911 2.7 RS, Porsche 911 Turbo, Aston Martin V8 Vantage.

*Lotus Turbo Esprit SE
(1989)*

Lotus Turbo Esprit
(1980–1992)

The Lotus Esprit has had a long and illustrious history dating back to when the car was first introduced in 1976. One of the most revered versions was the Turbo that first surfaced in 1980 and featured a four-cylinder aluminium engine that could produce 210 bhp. The Esprit's "credentials" were further enhanced thanks to a movie appearance – the Turbo was James Bond's vehicle of choice (both on the road and underwater) in *The Spy Who Loved Me*. Over the decades there have been numerous incarnations of the Esprit, but its production run (that spanned an incredible 28 years) came to a close on February 21st, 2004.

Specifications

ENGINE	2174 cc
MAX POWER	210 bhp at 6,250 rpm
MAX TORQUE	200 lb ft at 4,500 rpm
0-60 MPH (0-100 KM/H)	5.6 secs
TOP SPEED	150 mph (241 km/h)

Ferrari 288 GTO
(1984–1985)

The mid-engined GTO is actually the forefather of the classic F40, but this 1980s supercar has earned its rightful place in the history books because its body was manufactured from composite materials such as carbon fiber – making it one of the very few cars to feature such race-developed technology. These lightweight materials coupled with a twin-turbo 2.8-liter V8 engine meant that the GTO was an extremely quick car with handling that was, let's just say, best enjoyed by the experienced driver.

Ferrari 288 GTO specifications

ENGINE	2855 cc
MAX POWER	400 bhp at 7,000 rpm
MAX TORQUE	365 lb ft at 3,800 rpm
0-60 MPH (0-100 KM/H)	4.7 secs
TOP SPEED	188 mph (303 km/h)

Ferrari Testarossa specifications

ENGINE	4942 cc
MAX POWER	390 bhp at 6,300 rpm
MAX TORQUE	354 lb ft at 4,500 rpm
0-60 MPH (0-100 KM/H)	5.3 secs
TOP SPEED	180 mph (289 km/h)

Ferrari Testarossa
(1984–1992)

Aimed at being more of a GT than a hardcore road racer, the Testarossa ("Red Head") showed Ferrari heading in a more refined direction while retaining the astonishing speed and acceleration that all supercar owners demand. And the flat-12 engine saw to that with its 390 bhp.

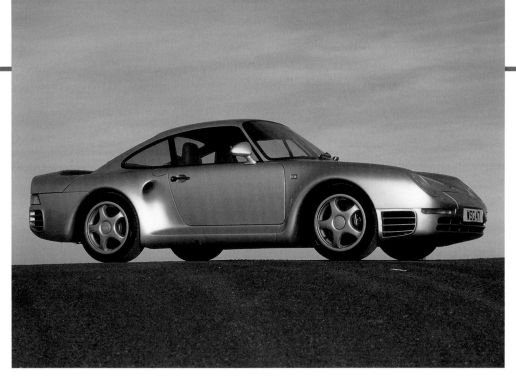

Other key cars from the 1980s:
Aston Martin Bulldog,
Aston Martin Vantage Zagato,
Ruf CTR Yellowbird.

Porsche 959
(1987–1991)

Trust Porsche to come up with the 959, able to hit 0-60 mph (0-100 km/h) in under 4 secs. This phenomenal acceleration was achieved using a rear-mounted twin-turbo flat-six engine that produced 450 bhp. To get such power down onto the road, the 959 featured four-wheel drive paired with a six-speed gearbox, and the kind of stability needed to hit a cool 197 mph (317 km/h).

Porsche 959 specifications	
ENGINE	2850 cc
MAX POWER	450 bhp at 6,500 rpm
MAX TORQUE	369 lb ft at 5,000 rpm
0-60 MPH (0-100 KM/H)	3.6 secs
TOP SPEED	197 mph (317 km/h)

Ferrari F40
(1987–1992)

Released to celebrate the company's 40th anniversary, the F40 was the last road car that the marque's creator, Enzo Ferrari, commissioned before he passed away – but what a swansong. It looked more like a racing car than a supercar and it featured a 2.9-liter V8 engine that would see a brave driver propelled to over 200 mph (322 km/h). The car is, of course, not for the faint-hearted but its position as one of the iconic supercars of any age is indisputable.

Ferrari F40 specifications	
ENGINE	2936 cc
MAX POWER	478 bhp at 7,000 rpm
MAX TORQUE	425 lb ft at 4,000 rpm
0-60 MPH (0-100 KM/H)	3.9 secs
TOP SPEED	201 mph (323 km/h)

Bugatti EB110
(1992–1995)

Bugatti EB110 specifications	
ENGINE	3500 cc
MAX POWER	603 bhp at 8,250 rpm
MAX TORQUE	479 lb ft at 4,250 rpm
0-60 MPH (0-100 KM/H)	3.1 secs
TOP SPEED	218 mph (351 km/h)

It was supposed to be the rebirth of the Bugatti brand and, at first, the future was looking bright for the marque. While the EB110's looks may have had mixed reviews, the Bugatti was a true supercar with staggering performance; it featured, thanks to the chassis and four-wheel drive, a colossal amount of grip to make the most out of all that power. Two versions were available – the humble GT with 553 bhp and the Supersport, which boasted 603 bhp. But alas, the Bugatti dream imploded in 1995 when the company went bust, mainly because of the global recession.

Jaguar XJ220
(1992–1994)

Jaguar XJ220 specifications	
ENGINE	2498 cc
MAX POWER	542 bhp at 6,500 rpm
MAX TORQUE	472 lb ft at 5,000 rpm
0-60 MPH (0-100 KM/H)	3.6 secs
TOP SPEED	210 mph+ (338 km/h)

Quite frankly, the Jaguar supercar was something of a debacle. Back in 1988 customers were bedazzled by promises of a huge V12 engine, coupled with a four-wheel drive, when the XJ220 prototype was unveiled. Down went the deposits as (very rich) people waited for the car's arrival in 1992. The trouble was that Jaguar replaced the engine with a V6 and dumped the four-wheel drive. Some angry customers withdrew their orders and demanded their deposits back; legal wranglings ensued. Add to this a world recession, and Jaguar's supercar foundered. The sad fact is that on its release, the XJ220 was still a fantastically fast car boasting supreme handling (in dry conditions) – and then there were those striking looks.

McLaren F1
(1993–1997)

McLaren F1 specifications	
ENGINE	6064 cc
MAX POWER	627 bhp at 7,400 rpm
MAX TORQUE	479 lb ft at 4,000 rpm
0-60 MPH (0-100 KM/H)	3.2 secs
TOP SPEED	240 mph (386 km/h)

Until recently, the McLaren F1 was the fastest car on the planet. Its BMW 6.1-liter V12 engine produced a staggering 627 bhp and could propel the car up to 240 mph (386 km/h). And never mind the 0–60 mph (0-100 km/h) time – the F1 could hit 100 mph (161 km/h) in just 6.3 secs. The key to the McLaren's success was the fact that it was created entirely from carbon fiber and built on a philosophy that demanded it be put together with absolute precision.

The resulting car can seat three people – the driver in the middle with two passengers to the side and back of him. The McLaren's production came to an end when customers decided that the price tag was perhaps stretching even them a little too much. The McLaren would also carve out a name for itself on the track by winning the Le Mans 24-hour race in 1995.

Ferrari F50
(1995-1997)

What happens when you put a Formula One engine into a production car? Well, trust Ferrari to be the ones bold enough to try it – and, of course, to get it right with the F50. The 4.7-liter V12 featured in the supercar was a direct descendant of the engine that nearly earned Alain Prost top honors in the 1990 F1 World Championship. Just as important to the F50's achievement as a true race car made for the road was its easy-to-access driving experience – the F50 left its forefather the F40 for dead on a twisty track, so sweet and accessible was its handling.

Ferrari F50 specifications

ENGINE	4698 cc
MAX POWER	513 bhp at 8,000 rpm
MAX TORQUE	347 lb ft at 6,500 rpm
0-60 MPH (0-100 KM/H)	3.7 secs
TOP SPEED	202 mph (325 km/h)

The Modern Supercar

Here is the culmination of what the best minds in the supercar business have to offer thanks to the last 50 years. From GTs through to roadsters, all the supercars featured here offer the true car-lover a wealth of treasures to indulge themselves in; looks that are intoxicating; performance that is G-force defying; and a driving experience that is truly unforgettable. Welcome to the state-of-the-supercar-art...

Aston Martin Vanquish S

The arrival of the original Vanquish and this, its more powerful brother the Vanquish S, has ushered in a new era for Britain's most iconic sports car company...

When Aston Martin unveiled the Vanquish in 2001, first impressions had to count – the Ford-owned company was coming out of the recession-ridden 1990s and needed an all-new flagship car to show the world that they were more than their classic DB7 coupe. Thanks to Ford's vision for the company and car designer maestro Ian Callum, jaws dropped to the floor when the car was first shown – the Vanquish was that striking; that poised; that menacing; that... British.

Featuring a V12 6-liter engine pumping out 460 bhp, those bold good looks were backed up with an equally impressive driving experience. Ford wanted Aston Martin to become the home of new car technology – the Vanquish featured a body combining both aluminium and carbon fiber, which was light enough to put itself in range of serious supercar territory.

But the car marque's crowning glory is the Vanquish S. Debuted at the Paris Motor Show, France, in 2004, the S is the fastest production model Aston Martin has ever made. The 48-valve V12 6-liter engine now produces 520 bhp over the previous Vanquish's 460 bhp, and it can top 200 mph (322 km/h). The S also features stiffer springs and dampers, plus shorter steering arms to give drivers the ultimate handling package.

24

"The Vanquish S is the fastest production model
Aston Martin has ever made."

From Start To Finish

It takes 396 hours for Aston Martin's engineers at the Newport Pagnall factory, in the UK, to hand-build the Vanquish S; the interior alone takes more than 70 hours to craft, and features eight hides of leather.

Nip And Tuck

Cosmetically the S has been given subtle tweaks over the original Vanquish; as well as changes to the car's nose, the design adds stability and balance while reducing lift.

What Lies Beneath

The Vanquish was always intended to show off Aston Martin as a hotbed of cutting-edge technology. This is perfectly reflected by the materials that make up the car – aluminium is used for the bulkheads and floor while the windshield pillars and center tunnel are made from carbon fiber.

Something Old, Something New

Designed by car industry legend Ian Callum, the Vanquish manages to blend perfectly the old and the new into a modern and fresh look. Callum is reported to have said that it was the DB4 GT Zagato from the 1960s that inspired his vision for the Vanquish.

Copyright Aston Martin

Copyright Aston Martin

Copyright Aston Martin

Aston Martin Vanquish S: The Specifications

ENGINE	Fuel injected 48-valve V12	STEERING	Rack and pinion with variable power assist	SUSPENSION REAR	Double wishbones with monutube dampers, coil
VALVETRAIN	DOHC 4 valves / cyl				springs & anti-roll bar
DISPLACEMENT	5935 cc	BRAKES FRONT	Ventilated & grooved with six callipers/	CURB WEIGHT	4,134 lbs/1,875 kg
MAXIMUM POWER	520 bhp at 7,000 rpm		14.5 in/370 mm	LENGTH	184 in/4,665 mm
MAXIMUM TORQUE	425 lb ft at 5,800 rpm	BRAKES REAR	Ventilated & grooved	WIDTH	76 in/1,923 mm
TRANSMISSION	Six-speed manual with paddle shifting		with four callipers/ 13 in/330 mm	HEIGHT	52 in/1,318 mm
0–60 MPH (0-100 KM/H)	4.7 secs			WHEELS FRONT	9 x 19 in
0–125 MPH (0-201 KM/H)	9.8 secs	SUSPENSION FRONT	Double wishbones with	WHEEL REAR	10 x 19 in
MAXIMUM SPEED	200 mph (322 km/h)+		monutube dampers, coil springs & anti-roll bar		

Aston Martin DB9

While the Vanquish showed the world where Aston Martin's future lay, it's the DB9 that has further secured Aston Martin's place as one of the most desirable brands on the planet...

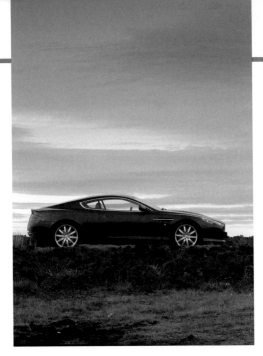

The DB7 was an iconic British car. The problem was that the DB7 had been around for a while and was beginning to show its age. It needed an all-new replacement – something that would stand up to Ferrari and Porsche; while the Vanquish demonstrated that Aston had its eye firmly on the future, the company still needed a lower priced car that would help it sell 5,000 cars a year. The DB9 is that car – built at Aston Martin's all-new factory in Gaydon, England, it is regarded as one of the greatest GTs ever built.

Its low, sleek and muscular looks can be credited to design maestro Ian Callum who handed over the baton to Henrik Fisker to complete what many argue is the most beautiful car on sale today. But the DB9's beauty isn't merely skin deep – under the exterior is a wholly new platform. Named the VH (Vertical and Horizontal), it's constructed from aluminium, and all the major mechanical and body components have been engineered from aluminium, magnesium or lightweight composite materials. This means that with its V12 450 bhp engine, the DB9 is able to propel itself at a fierce pace on the straights because of its relative lightness but also to corner confidently because of its rigidity. Most importantly, the driver never feels left out, or scared, by the DB9. This accessibility is easily managed by either a manual six-speed gearbox or a six-speed ZF automatic with paddle shifts that, while shaving 0.2 secs off the car's 0–60 mph (0-100 km/h) time, is highly regarded for its suppleness and smoothness.

29

"Many argue that the DB9 is the most beautiful car on sale today."

Punishing The Prototypes

53 DB9 prototypes were made and put through their paces to ensure that the cars could cut it in extreme climates – from the gruelling conditions of Death Valley and the Arctic Circle through to its mechanics being tested on the Nürburgring track in Germany.

Delight In The Details

The DB9's cockpit has a wealth of quality touches – the glass starter button in the center console shimmers red when the ignition is switched on, and once the engine is turned on the button lights up blue.

Personalized For Perfection

There are 29 colors available but Aston Martin will let you choose any you want at an extra cost. As well as a multitude of different leather options, four different woods are also available for the Aston's interior – mahogany, walnut, bamboo and piano black.

Taking A Different Tach

The rev counter featured in the DB9 actually runs counter-clockwise, which echoes early Aston Martins such as the Atom and DB2. You won't find a red line on the tachometer either – instead a red light appears once the maximum revs are hit.

Swan Song

The DB9's doors don't open like the average coupe's – they actually pull upward at a twelve-o'clock angle to help the driver gain easier access to the cabin.

Copyright Aston Martin

Copyright Aston Martin

Copyright Aston Martin

Aston Martin DB9: The Specifications

ENGINE	Fuel injected 48-valve V12	STEERING	Rack and pinion with Servotronic speed-sensitive power-assist	SUSPENSION REAR	Double wishbones with monutube dampers, coil springs & anti-roll bar
VALVETRAIN	DOHC 4 valves / cyl				
DISPLACEMENT	5935 cc				
MAXIMUM POWER	450 bhp at 6,000 rpm	BRAKES FRONT	Ventilated & grooved with six callipers/ 14 in/355 mm	CURB WEIGHT	3,770 lbs/1,710 kg (manual) 3,968 lbs/1,800 kg (auto)
MAXIMUM TORQUE	420 lb ft at 5,000 rpm				
TRANSMISSION	Six-speed manual or six-speed auto	BRAKES REAR	Ventilated & grooved with four callipers/ 13 in/330 mm	LENGTH	185 in/4,710 mm
0–60 MPH (0-100 KM/H)	4.7 secs (manual) 4.9 secs (auto)			WIDTH	74 in/1,875 mm
		SUSPENSION FRONT	Double wishbones with monutube dampers, coil springs & anti-roll bar	HEIGHT	50 in/1,270 mm
0–125 MPH (0-201 KM/H)	4.9 secs (manual) 5.1 secs (auto)			WHEELS FRONT	8.5 x19 in
				WHEEL REAR	9.5 x 19 in
MAXIMUM SPEED	186 mph (199 km/h)				

Aston Martin DBR9

Aston Martin has wanted to return to the international motor racing scene for decades and this is how they are doing it – with the DBR9. Based on the DB9 and featuring the same aluminium chassis, the racing car has had some major modifications to make sure it's up to the job of winning major competitions.

The DBR9's engine produces 600 bhp compared to the DB9's 450 bhp while the suspension set-up boasts up-rated components plus a revised geometry. The car now features carbon brakes and a six-speed sequential gearbox mounted on the rear axle. The DBR9's aerodynamics have been optimized to produce the best possible performance on the track, and the panels of the racer are also handmade from carbon fiber composite to ensure the car meets competition weight regulations.

The DBR9 experienced major success on its debut at the 53rd Annual 12 Hours of Sebring, Florida in March 2005, where Aston's team gleaned itself a GT1 class victory.

Aston Martin V8 Vantage

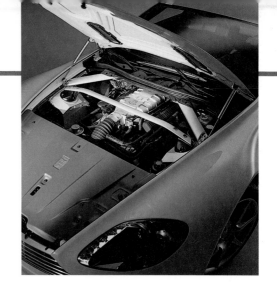

This is what everyone is calling the new "baby" Aston, but it's destined to make one very big splash when it finally touches down...

It could be argued that the V8 Vantage is the single most important Aston ever to be built. It's the most affordable Aston to be made available to the masses with a price that puts it in line with the likes of the Porsche 911.

That's virgin territory for Aston Martin, but they are all set to hit the mark. Using their unique aluminium VH platform, as used by the DB9 but shortened with stiffer suspension, the V8 Vantage has a howling 4.3-liter engine providing the firepower. While the V8 Vantage "only" features a V8, it can match the V12-driven DB9 because it's lighter – giving it a 0–60 mph (0-100 km/h) time of 4.8 secs and a top speed of 175 mph (282 km/h).

Unsurprisingly of course, the interior of the two-seater is up to the typical Aston high standards – the alloy fascia with instrument panel features beautifully finished aluminium. But optional mahogany, walnut or bamboo can be included.

As for the build quality, 78 prototypes have been clocking up 1,500,000 miles between them. The Nürburgring, Germany, and the Nardo test track, Italy, have been used to develop and hone the V8 Vantage's handling. In fact, one V8 Vantage was challenged with the task of racking up 5,000 miles round the Nürburgring, which it did without breaking its stride.

"The Aston Martin V8 Vantage is exotica defined, and put up against its competitors you have to ask yourself – which one is the more desirable?

Which one has that 'X factor' which elevates it beyond mere sports car?

The answer is staring you in the face..."

Wait-y Issues...

To make sure the V8 Vantage kept that important air of exclusivity, production of the car was capped at 2,500 per year. Potential buyers could expect epic waiting lists.

Designer Departed

The good-looking V8 Vantage was designed by Henrik Fisker (who also designed the DB9). He has since departed Aston Martin and moved to California to set up an automotive design and customization company.

Weight A Minute...

The front-engined V8 Vantage has the spot-on weight distribution and offers the ideal set-up for any self-respecting sports car. The Aston's dry-sump lubrication system means that the engine can be placed lower in the body, meaning a lower center of gravity. The result – better balance and stability.

Aston Martin V8 Vantage: The Specifications

ENGINE	All alloy quad overhead camshaft 32 valve V8	BRAKES FRONT	Ventilated & grooved steel discs with four-piston monobloc callipers/ 14 in/355 mm, ABS	SUSPENSION REAR	Independent double aluminium wishbones with coil over aluminium monutube dampers & anti-roll bar
VALVETRAIN	DOHC 4 valves / cyl				
DISPLACEMENT	4280 cc				
MAXIMUM POWER	380 bhp at 7,000 rpm	BRAKES REAR	Ventilated & grooved steel discs with four-piston monobloc callipers/ 13 in/330 mm, ABS		
MAXIMUM TORQUE	302 lb ft at 5,000 rpm			CURB WEIGHT	3,461 lbs/1,570 kg
TRANSMISSION	Six-speed manual			LENGTH	173 in/4,383 mm
0–60 MPH (0-100 KM/H)	4.8 secs			WIDTH	73 in/1,866 mm
MAXIMUM SPEED	175 mph (282 km/h)	SUSPENSION FRONT	Independent double aluminium wishbones with coil over aluminium monutube dampers & anti-roll bar	HEIGHT	49 in/1,255 mm
STEERING	Rack and pinion with power assist			WHEELS FRONT	8.5 x 18 in
				WHEEL REAR	9.5 x 18 in

B Engineering Edonis

When Bugatti crashed and burned in the 1990s, a small group of ex-employees decided to take their destiny into their own hands and produce a supercar...

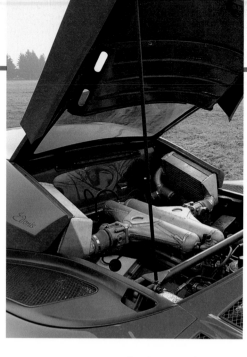

The Edonis is unusual. Not just in the way it looks with its bizarre lines and curves. The company behind this supercar isn't interested in becoming a major player. All B Engineering ever wanted the supercar to be was a showcase for cutting-edge technology that represented the excellence of both the company and the region where it is built – Modena, Italy, home of the supercar.

The number of staff may be small but many have worked for some of the greatest supercar makers of all time – Ferrari, Lamborghini and Maserati, to name but a few. In fact, the owner of the company, Jean-Marc Borel, used to be the vice chairman of Bugatti.

B Engineering's links with Bugatti form the core of the Edonis – when Bugatti declared bankruptcy in 1995, 21 leftover carbon fiber tubs from the Bugatti EB110 were acquired by B Engineering to create the Edonis. At the heart of the car's hand-built aluminium body is an extreme engine, an evolution of the EB110's – a 3.7-liter V12 with twin turbochargers, plus a six-speed manual gearbox.

With project director, Nicola Materazzi, who is famous for the classic handling of the Ferrari, it's perhaps predictable that the Edonis should become renowned for its precision steering and abundant feel.

43

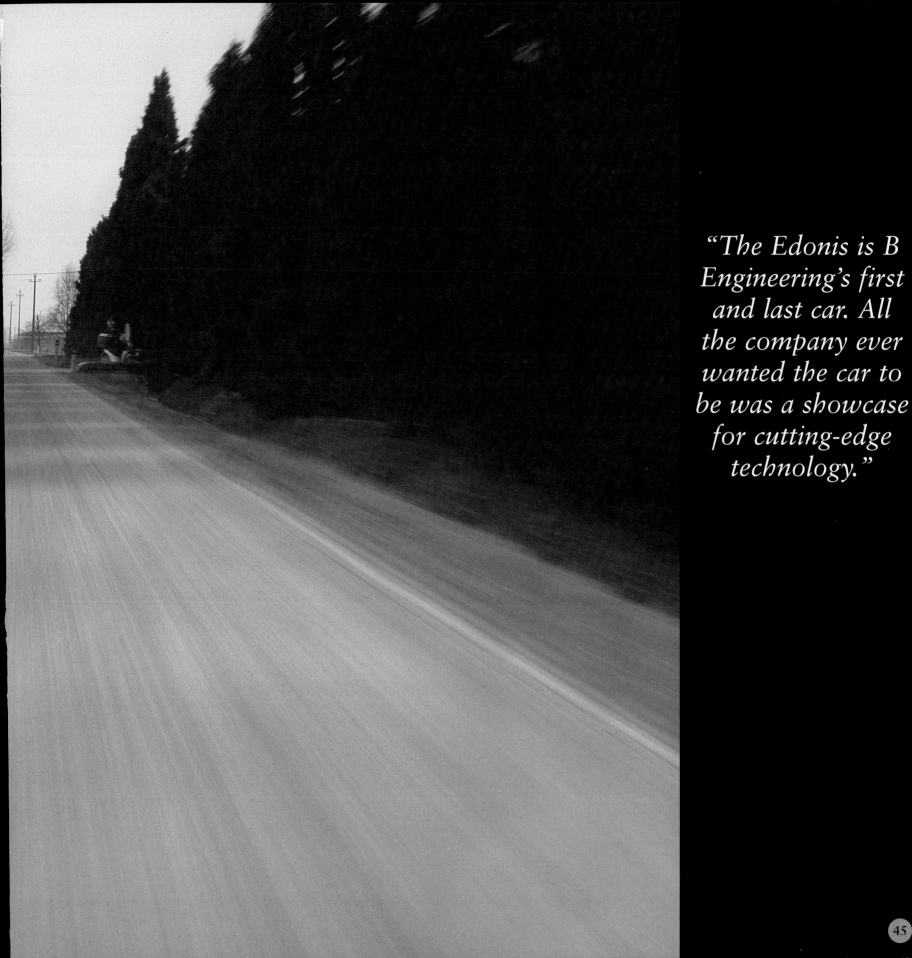

"The Edonis is B Engineering's first and last car. All the company ever wanted the car to be was a showcase for cutting-edge technology."

Record Breaker

A 720 bhp version of the Edonis managed to break the circuit record of the Nardo race circuit in Italy by lapping at 223 mph (359 km/h).

Named And Famed

The word Edonis is actually the Greek word for pleasure. And only a select few will be privileged enough to experience the car – just 21 will be made. B Engineering decided to make 21 because the Edonis is the first car of the 21st century.

Keeping It In The Family

B Engineering has stayed true to its vision of creating a supercar that uses all the incredible resources of the Modena area – local body builders, casters, upholsterers, pattern makers and others were called in to produce the Edonis.

Perfect Supercar CV

The Edonis's project director, Nicola Materazzi, has a resumé that screams supercar pioneer – he was the main contractor for the likes of Bugatti, and then from 1980, he worked for Ferrari on projects such as the GTO Evoluzione and F40. He was also top dog at Ferrari's F1 research and design division.

gineering Edonis (720 bhp version): The Specifications

E	Twin turbocharged V12	MAXIMUM SPEED	223 mph (359 km/h)	SUSPENSION REAR	Double wishbon
TRAIN	DOHC, 5 valves / cyl	STEERING	Rack and pinion with		coil springs, gas
CEMENT	3760 cc		power assist		& anti-roll bar
UM POWER	720 bhp at 8,000 rpm	BRAKES FRONT	Cross-drilled & ventilated	CURB WEIGHT	3,307 lbs/1,500
UM TORQUE	590 lb ft at 5,250 rpm		discs, ABS/13 in/335 mm	LENGTH	171 in/4,350 mm
MISSION	Six-speed manual	BRAKES REAR	Cross-drilled & ventilated	WIDTH	79 in/1,998 mm
PH (0-100 KM/H)	4 secs		discs, ABS/13 in/335 mm	HEIGHT	44 in/1,120 mm
		SUSPENSION FRONT	Double wishbones with		
PH (0-161 KM/H)	8.2 secs		coil springs, gas dampers		
			& anti-roll bar		

Ferrari Enzo

Is it beauty or the beast? It doesn't really matter, the Enzo defines what the supercar moniker is all about...

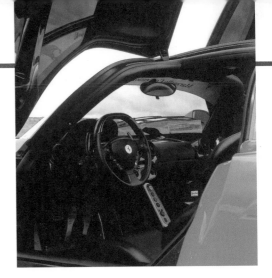

Explosive, aggressive, uncompromising. Named after the company's founder Enzo Ferrari, who died in 1988, the Enzo is the marque's fastest ever road car with a top speed of over 217 mph (349 km/h), and the looks created by Pininfarina are pure Formula One drama. That F1 nose, the angular body and those venturis shout to even the most casual of observers that this car is the closest a driver will ever get to feeling like Michael Schumacher. With 660 bhp produced by an ultra lightweight aluminium 6-liter V12 engine, the Enzo can devour many of its modern day competitors with a 0–60 mph (0-100 km/h) time of 3.5 secs.

Ferrari has made sure that the Enzo makes the most of its gigantic power by using its hi-tech ASR traction control system and an F1-style six-speed paddle shift that can snap through the gears in milliseconds. The Enzo's handling is legendary as well – its chassis is constructed from carbon fiber and Kevlar honeycomb, which provides the Enzo with its extreme rigidity and strength; while that F1 nose, with its three air intakes, helps to keep the car glued to the road as it increases in speed, while keeping the V12 cool. Stopping capability is vital for such explosive thrust – and the carbon ceramic brakes with ABS are more than a match for such a punishing job.

Open the Enzo's scissor doors and there's easy access to the carbon fiber and leather cabin. The steering wheel has a multitude of F1-style buttons mounted on it for controlling everything from race settings to turning off the ASR. And for that extra Grand Prix touch, there are LEDs running along the top of the wheel, which act as a rev counter.

"*The Enzo is Ferrari's fastest ever road car with a top speed of over 217 mph.*"

Going, Going, Gone

Like any respectable supercar, limiting the numbers that can be bought is paramount. Initially, only 349 Enzos were made to order, and Ferrari sold every single one of them before they'd even shown a single picture or spec list of the car. The final figure for the number of Enzos assembled is 400 – one more than planned, with the extra car being auctioned off to raise money for the 2004 Asian tsunami victims.

F1 Champ Elevates Enzo

Formula One champion Michael Schumacher had a firm hand in developing the Enzo. He drove several prototypes of the supercar and gave his thoughts on all aspects of the Enzo, from its performance to the driving position. In fact, thanks to Schumacher, there are 16 different pedal settings available to choose from.

Sky's The Limit

It would appear that the Enzo's value doesn't depreciate. If you want proof – in 2004, the Enzo became eBay Motors' most expensive car ever sold when a Swiss man (bidding from Brazil) paid a premium.

Ferrari Enzo: The Specifications

ENGINE	Aluminium V12	**STEERING**	Rack and pinion with power assist	**SUSPENSION REAR**	Double wishbones with pushrod links, coil springs, gas dampers & anti-rollbar
VALVETRAIN	DOHC, 4 valves / cyl with continuously variable timing	**BRAKES FRONT**	Ventilated carbon-ceramic discs with 6-pot callipers, ABS/15 in/380 mm		
DISPLACEMENT	5988 cc			**CURB WEIGHT**	3,009 lbs/1,365 kg
MAXIMUM POWER	660 bhp at 7,800 rpm	**BRAKES REAR**	Ventilated carbon-ceramic discs with 4-pot callipers, ABS/15 in/380 mm	**LENGTH**	185 in/4,702 mm
MAXIMUM TORQUE	485 lb ft at 5,500 rpm			**WIDTH**	80 in/2,035 mm
TRANSMISSION	Six-speed sequential			**HEIGHT**	45 in/1,147 mm
0–60 MPH (0-100 KM/H)	3.5 secs	**SUSPENSION FRONT**	Double wishbones with pushrod links, coil springs, gas dampers & anti-roll bar	**WHEELS FRONT**	9 x 19 in
0–125 MPH (0-201 KM/H)	6.5 secs			**WHEELS REAR**	12 x 19 in
MAXIMUM SPEED	217 mph+ (349 km/h)				

Ferrari F430

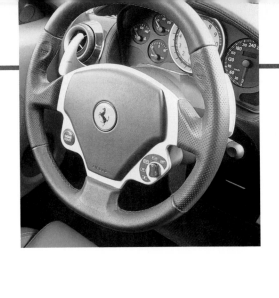

The Lamborghini Gallardo, the Ford GT and the Aston Martin V8 Vantage... yes, Ferrari may have been facing increased competition over the past couple of years but trust them to come out fighting...

The F430 had a tough act to follow – Ferrari's illustrious reputation for creating exceptional sports coupes is unrivalled. Designed by Pininfarina, the 360 Modena replacement is a masterclass in mixing the sensual with the angular, and blending such seemingly diametric elements into a alluring body shape.

The successor to the acclaimed 360, the F430 is constructed entirely from aluminium and features a brand new 4.3-liter V8 engine that boasts far more torque than its forebearer and produces 483 bhp – the car has a 0–62 time of 4 secs and a top speed of 195 mph (314 km/h). The F430 features a six-speed manual as standard and, as an option, a F1 paddleshift that can now move through those gears quicker than the previous incarnation found in the 360.

The F430 also has some new Formula One-sourced tricks up its sleeve for the driver to indulge in. The "manettino" – which is a switch that can be flicked between various different modes – Ice, Wet, Sport, Race and CST – and lets you, with a simple flick, automatically alter the F430's settings such as dampers, traction control plus the speed of the F1 gearshifts.

The F430 also features an electronic differential. This e-diff aids torque distribution to the rear wheels, so if over-keen driving sees the back end starting to slide out, the clutches inside the e-diff quickly send torque to the wheel that has the most traction. Thanks to this unique e-diff, the F430 has been acclaimed for its benign handling and the ability to conquer corners with absolute and utter controllable ease.

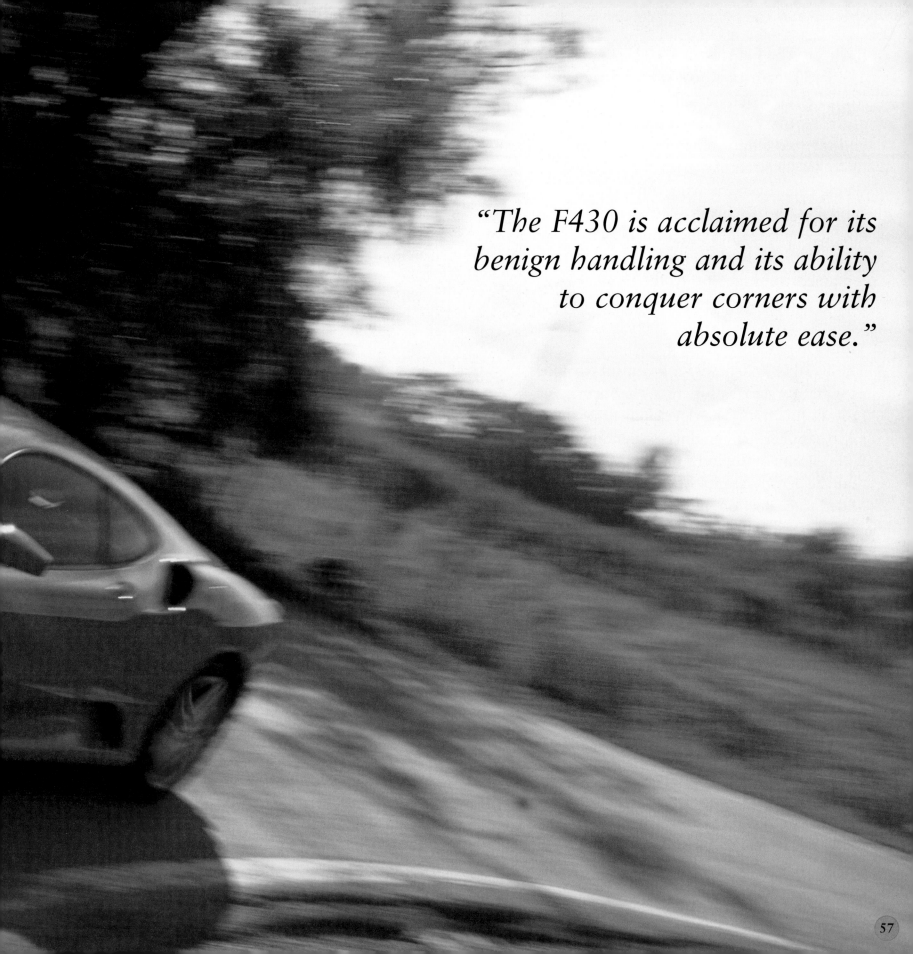

"*The F430 is acclaimed for its benign handling and its ability to conquer corners with absolute ease.*"

Back To The Future

The F430 features a host of styling cues from Ferrari's rich heritage – the air scoops at the rear pay homage to the 250 LM's, and the two elliptical air intakes at the front are inspired by Ferrari's 1961 F1 racing cars. Even the wing mirrors are similar to the Testarossa of the 1980s. Of course, the Enzo heavily influences the rear layout – the only elements that have remained from the 360 to the F430 are the doors, hood and roof.

Wind Up

The F430 is undeniably a beautiful car but, as with any serious supercar, the form follows function. The development of the F430 saw Ferrari's engineers spending over 2,000 hours in a wind tunnel making sure that the aerodynamics of the car were honed to perfection.

A Big Downer

The F430 features a 50 percent increase in downforce when compared to its successor, the 360 Modena. That means stability and safety at high speeds is now vastly improved.

Devil In The Details

Ferrari want owners to spread the word about the F430 to their hearts content. Not only can customers turn up with a color sample that they want their car painted in but they can also decide on the tiny details, such as the thread color used inside the car and even the spacing of the actual stitching.

Ferrari F430: The Specifications

ENGINE	Aluminium V8	STEERING	Rack and pinion with power assist		adjustable tube shocks & anti-roll bar
VALVETRAIN	DOHC, 4 valves / cyl with variable timing and variable intake tract	BRAKES FRONT	Carbon-ceramic discs (optional) with 6-piston callipers/15 in/380 mm, ABS, EBD	SUSPENSION REAR	Double wishbones with coil springs, electrically adjustable tube shocks
DISPLACEMENT	4308 cc				& anti-roll bar
MAXIMUM POWER	483 bhp at 8,500 rpm				
MAXIMUM TORQUE	343 lb ft at 5,250 rpm	BRAKES REAR	Carbon-ceramic discs (optional), 4-piston callipers/14 in/350 mm, ABS, EBD	CURB WEIGHT	3,197 lbs/1,450 kg
TRANSMISSION	Six-speed manual (optional F1 paddleshift available)			LENGTH	178 in/4,512 mm
				WIDTH	76 in/1,923 mm
				HEIGHT	48 in/1,214 mm
0–60 MPH (0-100 KM/H)	4 secs	SUSPENSION FRONT	Double wishbones with coil springs, electrically	WHEELS FRONT	7.5 x 19 in
MAXIMUM SPEED	196 mph (315 km/h)			WHEEL REAR	10 x 19 in

Ford GT

The Ferrari-beating Le Mans racing legend is reborn and the motoring world falls in love all over again...

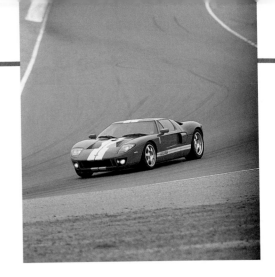

The GT40's legacy was talked about for decades to come. But fast forward to the Detroit Auto Show in 2002 – where the concept of its successor was unveiled – and everyone started talking again. The world did a double take, pinched itself to make sure that it wasn't dreaming and then pulled out its checkbook.

Sitting close to the ground on its low profile tires, the GT epitomizes how a proper sports car should look and, with a Ford-claimed 500 bhp nestled behind the driver, how it should go as well. With a 0–60 mph (0-100 km/h) time of 3.7 secs and a top speed of 200 mph (322 km/h), this is no lukewarm or cynical attempt to cash-in on Ford's heritage.

The GT may look dimensionally like the original at first glance but the car is actually 3.3 inches (84 mm) taller than its forbearer, and it's wider. And underneath that fine looking exterior is a thoroughly modern all-aluminium spaceframe. Providing the fireworks is a supercharged 5.4-liter V8 mid-engine lump with enough torque to rip tarmac from the road. Or at the very least, rip the rubber off those 19 in tires on the back. After all, the Ford features no traction control or fancy stability systems; driver and passenger air bags and anti-lock brakes are the only concessions to modern "safe" motoring.

The car is renowned for being an absolute cinch to drive through rush hour as well as at full speed. Unlike some of its more highly strung supercar competitors, this car also enjoys being on the limit, and with the GT's chassis, spot-on steering and entertaining handling, has the driving experience to match those fine looks too.

"The original GT40 was a beautiful car; but the Ford GT is quite simply stunning."

As Good As Old

Like the exterior, the GT's cockpit is a modern take on the old GT40 featuring toggle switches, seats with ventilated seat backs and squabs, and a speedo located above the transmission tunnel.

Fast Forward

To make sure that the GT was ready for their centennial celebrations in 2003, Ford managed to turn the concept car into a production model in a record-breaking 16 months.

Last In Line

Of the 5,000 GTs made, Ford allowed only 85 cars to be shipped over to Europe. The poor old UK had only 24 allocated – so you can only begin to imagine the scrambling of potential purchasers as they tried to get on the fabled shortlist.

The Past Made New

The GT is actually part of Ford's Living Legends range – cars from yester-year given a fresh reworking. Other cars in the series include the glorious-looking Ford Mustang and Thunderbird.

Size Matters

The original GT40 was named so because it was 40 inches (1,016 mm) tall. The GT has crept up in height to accommodate taller drivers and now stands at 43.3 inches (1,100 mm). The height difference aside, if you're wondering why Ford didn't simply stick with GT40 as the name, well, it's because they don't actually own the copyright to it.

Ford GT: The Specifications

ENGINE	Aluminium V8	STEERING	Rack and pinion with power assist		adjustable tube shocks & anti-roll bar
VALVETRAIN	DOHC, 4 valves / cyl with variable timing and variable intake tract	BRAKES FRONT	Carbon-ceramic discs (optional) with 6-piston callipers/15 in/380 mm, ABS, EBD	SUSPENSION REAR	Double wishbones with coil springs, electrically adjustable tube shocks & anti-roll bar
DISPLACEMENT	4308 cc				
MAXIMUM POWER	483 bhp at 8,500 rpm				
MAXIMUM TORQUE	343 lb ft at 5,250 rpm	BRAKES REAR	Carbon-ceramic discs (optional), 4-piston callipers/14 in/350 mm, ABS, EBD	CURB WEIGHT	3,197 lbs/1,450 kg
TRANSMISSION	Six-speed manual (optional F1 paddleshift available)			LENGTH	178 in/4,512 mm
				WIDTH	76 in/1,923 mm
				HEIGHT	48 in/1,214 mm
0–60 MPH (0-100 KM/H)	4 secs	SUSPENSION FRONT	Double wishbones with coil springs, electrically	WHEELS FRONT	7.5 x 19 in
MAXIMUM SPEED	196 mph (315 km/h)			WHEEL REAR	10 x 19 in

Ford GT (2003)

Ford GT40
(1966 Le Mans)

Honda NSX

A supercar? From Japan? If you think that only the Europeans make supercars, think again. Honda has been producing one of the world's finest for the past 15 years...

The mid-engined, rear-wheel drive aluminium-bodied NSX is remarkable. Designed with extensive help from the world's greatest Formula One driver, Ayrton Senna, the car was launched in 1990 to critical acclaim.

As with all Honda VTECs, using the full range of the engine rewards the driver with a frenzy of power the higher up the rev range they go. This power delivery is coupled with a rewarding chassis that offers huge grip and balance.

While exotic supercars can demand deep pockets for maintenence the NSX is Japanese. Honda knows how to put a car together whether it be a 1.4 liter Civic or a 276 bhp supercar.

The current NSX was introduced in 2002 and has seen the original's pop-up headlamps replaced by fixed headlamps. The current car also has two engines to choose from – the 3.2-liter V6 with a six-speed manual producing 276 bhp, and the 3-liter V6 F-Matic version that produces 256 bhp.

"*The NSX – designed with extensive help from the world's greatest Formula One driver, Ayrton Senna*"

Senna Sense

While Ayrton Senna was over in Japan in 1989, he was asked to drive a prototype of the original NSX to glean his expert thoughts. According to Honda, he told their engineers: "I'm not sure I can really give you appropriate advice on a mass-production car, but I feel it's a little fragile." Because of that input, the Honda team ended up increasing the car's rigidity by 50 percent.

Convertable

The NSX is available with a targa top roof as well – the NSX-T – but critics do say that this affects the car's rigidity and that purists should stick to the coupe version.

World First

The NSX was the first production car in the world to feature all-aluminium construction for the chassis and suspension components, and it is still the only true mid-engine two-seater supercar to come out of the Land of the Rising Sun.

Fighting Talk

The NSX's sleek looks have their origins in the air, not on the road. The original sketches drawn up for the supercar were actually based on an F16 fighter jet.

Hand-Assembled Heaven

The NSX is hand-assembled in Japan. To make sure the engineers are good enough to put together the supercar, they have to go through a rigorous testing process before being allowed to work on the NSX.

Honda NSX Coupe 3.2 V6 / Acura NSX: The Specifications

ENGINE	24-valve V6	STEERING	Rack and pinion with Servotronic speed-sensitive power-assist	SUSPENSION REAR	Double wishbones with monutube dampers, coil springs & anti-roll bar
VALVETRAIN	DOHC VTEC 4 valves / cyl				
DISPLACEMENT	3179 cc				
MAXIMUM POWER	276 bhp at 7,300 rpm	BRAKES FRONT	Ventilated & grooved with six callipers/ 14 in/355 mm	CURB WEIGHT	3,770 lbs/1,710 kg (manual) 3,968 lbs/1,800 kg (auto)
MAXIMUM TORQUE	220 lb ft at 5,300 rpm				
TRANSMISSION	Six-speed manual or six-speed Auto				
		BRAKES REAR	Ventilated & grooved with 4 callipers/ 13 in/330 mm	LENGTH	174 in/4,430 mm
0–60 MPH (0-100 KM/H)	5.7 secs (manual) 4.9 secs (auto)			WIDTH	71 in/1,810 mm
		SUSPENSION FRONT	Double wishbones with monutube dampers, coil springs & anti-roll bar	HEIGHT	46 in/1,160 mm
0–100 MPH (0-161 KM/H)	4.9 secs (manual) 5.1 secs (auto)			WHEELS FRONT	7 x 17 in
				WHEEL REAR	9 x 17 in
MAXIMUM SPEED	168 mph (270 km/h)				

Koenigsegg CC

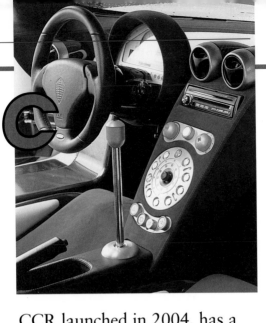

Ferociously fast, perfectly composed and luxurious... ladies and gentlemen, meet Sweden's McLaren F1 slayer with the world's most unpronounceable name...

Made in Sweden, the Koenigsegg CC, the dark horse of the supercar world, first broke cover in 2000. The car is the brainchild of Christian von Koenigsegg who set up the supercar project back in 1993 with a small, dedicated group of enthusiasts.

With its latest incarnations, the CC8S and the CCR, that power is now the stuff of legend – the top of the range CCR is officially the fastest production car in the world and can propel you to McLaren F1-vanquishing speeds of beyond 242 mph (389 km/h). The chassis, made from carbon fiber composite, is renowned for its communicative feedback whether the car's hurtling along at 200 mph (322 km/h) plus, or being threaded through pot-holed city streets.

While the base model – the CC8S – offers 655 bhp, its big brother, the CCR launched in 2004, has a staggering 806 bhp on tap and can make the dash from 0–62 in only 3.2 secs. This extreme version of the Koenigsegg is achieved by boosting the standard 4.7-liter V8 engine with a bi-compressor centrifugal supercharging system.

As well as a full leather interior and CD player, the driver can indulge in luxuries such as GPS navigation, a rear-view camera, a telephone system and even bespoke suitcases. Open-air thrills are also available because the car comes with a removable roof panel that can be stored under the front hood.

Yes, the price tag is a huge amount of cash – but the Koenigsegg is worth every penny.

"A truly remarkable supercar and virtually unbeatable; never has the phrase 'from zero to hero' been quite so true."

Full House
The Koenigsegg headquarters are housed in a large fighter jet facility and there are 30 full-time staff. At the moment, seven vehicles can be assembled simultaneously, and one car – bearing in mind there are 300-plus carbon fiber parts per car – takes 1,000 hours to assemble.

Door To Door
The carbon fiber doors of the CC open by swinging upward and resting at a 90° angle. Thanks to gas struts, this operation can be done with a gentle push and also means that the car is easily accessible even in confined spaces.

Record Breaker
In the 2004 edition of the *Guinness Book of Records*, the Koenigsegg CC8S is listed as the most powerful production car on the face of the planet. This has now been smashed by the 806 bhp CCR.

Have Car, Wheel Travel
The five-spoke magnesium alloy rims featured on the CCR have been specifically designed for Koenigsegg, and the tires are guaranteed to withstand the strains and stresses of traveling at over 240 mph (386 km/h).

Not Too Hot To Handle?
The engineers at Koenigsegg have implemented KACS (Koenigsegg Advanced Control System) as standard on the CCR – this allows the driver to adjust the car's suspension, aerodynamics, road holding and braking.

Koenigsegg CCR: The Specifications

ENGINE	V8 cast aluminium, supercharged	**BRAKES FRONT**	Ventilated with six-piston light alloy callipers, ABS/14 in/362 mm	**SUSPENSION REAR**	Double wishbones, adjustable VPS custom racing shock absorbers, pushrod operated & anti-roll bar
VALVETRAIN	DOHC 4 valves / cyl	**BRAKES REAR**	Ventilated with six-piston callipers/14 in/362 mm		
DISPLACEMENT	4700 cc				
MAXIMUM POWER	806 bhp at 6,900 rpm	**SUSPENSION FRONT**	Double wishbones, adjustable VPS custom racing shock absorbers, pushrod operated & anti-roll bar	**CURB WEIGHT**	2,711 lb/1,230 kg
MAXIMUM TORQUE	678 lb ft at 5,700 rpm			**LENGTH**	164 in/4,190 mm
TRANSMISSION	Six-speed manual			**WIDTH**	78 in/1,990 mm
0–60 MPH (0-100 KM/H)	5.9 secs			**HEIGHT**	42 in/1,070 mm
0–100 MPH (0-161 KM/H)	11.9 secs			**WHEELS FRONT**	9.5 x 19 in
MAXIMUM SPEED	242 mph+ (389 km/h)			**WHEEL REAR**	12.5 x 20 in
STEERING	Rack and pinion with power assist				

Lamborghini Murcielago

German build quality partnered with Italian passion... it's an intriguing concept but one that has paid off for the raging bull...

While Audi has ensured that the car has improved safety features and is better built than its predecessors, the Murcielago still has more than enough go to put a cold sweat on the foreheads of even the most experienced driver when taking the car to the limit.

The engine alone will see to that – with 580 bhp, the aluminium 6.2-liter V12 is blisteringly quick, and with its four-wheel drive with a central vicious coupler plus traction control, the steel and carbon fiber-built Lamborghini's huge power can be placed down on the road with more ease than its predecessors. The Murcielago also represents a first for the Lamborghini with the inclusion of a six-speed manual gearbox.

The car's rear spoiler adjusts depending on the speed, and those fabulous air intakes mounted on the car's rear shoulders open and close to cool the mammoth engine.

And for the show-offs, there's also a dash-mounted button to activate that Variable Air-flow Cooling System.

While the aggressive, melodramatic styling of previous Lamborghinis looked like testosterone wrought in metal, the more subtle Murcielago still demands your attention with its clean, simple and muscular lines – it's a thoroughly modern reimagining of the Lamborghini spirit penned by Belgian designer Luc Donckerwolcke.

It's with this new mindset – the passion of Lamborghini and the build quality of Audi – that the company has matured into a true 21st century supercar marque.

"The Murcielago demands your attention with its clean, simple and muscular lines. It's a thoroughly modern reimagining of the Lamborghini spirit."

What's In A Name?

The Murcielago is named after a bull that fought with the famous matador Rafael Molina "Lagartijo" on October 5, 1879. The aforementioned bull fought so bravely – and withstood being stabbed 24 times – that the great matador decided to honor the bull and spare its life. The bull was given to a top breeder and the Murcielago lineage continues to this day.

Bullet Proof?

Build quality and reliability were issues that sometimes hovered over the Lamborghinis of old. The now Audi-owned company say that Murcielagos are being driven over 10,000 miles a year by some customers with no problems.

Off With Its Head

Unlike the Diablo Roadster, which horrified the critics on its release, the Murcielago Roadster has taken their breaths away – not only incredible to look at but also a true zero-compromise supercar as well.

All-Wheel Thrills

Lamborghini wanted all the Murcielago's power put firmly down on the road so the driver could enjoy it, and not simply destroy the car's tires. Subsequently, any excess torque on the rear axle is moved to the front axle to aid the Murcielago in getting the best traction.

Lamborghini Murcielago: The Specifications

ENGINE VALVETRAIN	Aluminium alloy V12 DOHC, 4 valves / cyl with variable-geometry intake system and variable valve timing	0–125 MPH (0-201 KM/H)	8.6 secs	SUSPENSION REAR	Double wishbones with coil springs, gas dampers & anti-roll bar
		MAXIMUM SPEED	205 mph (330 km/h)		
		STEERING	Rack and pinion with power assist		
				CURB WEIGHT	3,638 lbs/1,650 kg
DISPLACEMENT	6,192 cc	BRAKES FRONT	Vented discs with 4-pot callipers, ABS/14 in/355 mm	LENGTH	180 in/4,580 mm
MAXIMUM POWER	580 bhp at 7,500 rpm			WIDTH	80 in/2,045 mm
MAXIMUM TORQUE	479 lb ft at 5,400 rpm	BRAKES REAR	Vented Discs with 4-pot callipers, ABS/335 mm	HEIGHT	45 in/1,135 mm
TRANSMISSION	Six-speed manual / Optional E-Gear			WHEELS FRONT	8.5 x 18 in
		SUSPENSION FRONT	Double wishbones with coil springs, gas dampers & anti-roll bar	WHEEL REAR	13 x 18 in
0–60 MPH (0-100 KM/H)	3.8 secs				

Lamborghini Gallardo

So, you can't afford a Murcielago? There's no need to worry because its baby brother is just as convincing...

That commute has never been quite so much fun – indeed, this car is easy to manage in the chaos of the rush hour but like any Lamborghini, the Gallardo is designed to be

pushed, and heavy-footing the accelerator shows that this bull hasn't lost its horns. That V10 bellows its way up the rev range, easily managed with the six-speed manual or the optional e-Gear sequential gear shifting system that lets the driver flick through the paddles mounted on the steering column.

This power is delivered by a mid-mounted V10 5-liter engine, which produces 493 bhp. The

Gallardo won't disappoint with a 0-62 time of 4.2 secs and a top speed of 192 mph (309 km/h). If anything, there's almost too much power on offer – finding a road long (and legal) enough to work your way up the gears is nearly impossible.

With its fully adjustable, electrically operated leather seats, there are enough creature comforts, such as air-conditioning and even optional satellite navigation, for the long-distance driver. The only blot on the landscape is actually accessing that cabin, which may disappoint if you are expecting scissor doors that sweep elegantly up into the air. No, these are, dare we say, just hinged conventional doors.

What's most striking about the Gallardo is just how successful Lamborghini has been at muscling its way into traditional Ferrari territory without any compromise in Lamborghini's philosophy.

"The Gallardo is designed to be pushed, and heavy-footing the accelerator shows that this bull hasn't lost its horns."

Winging It

The Gallardo's rear wing is able to change its angle depending on how quickly the car is moving. Below 50 mph (80 km/h), the wing remains flush with the rest of the Gallardo's bodywork but at 80 mph (129 km/h), it shifts upward to create more downforce. After all, with 500 bhp, the Gallardo needs all the stability it can get.

The Lamborghini A8?

Audi didn't just stipulate the Gallardo's build quality, they also lent their air-conditioning system and stereo; you can normally find them residing in the Audi A8. This might be a cost-cutting exercise for Lamborghini but, at the end of the day, both of the Audi elements are of a very high quality, so Gallardo owners needn't be disappointed.

Instant Hit

It's a blessing for any keen driver who's just taken delivery of their new pride and joy – unlike many cars, the Gallardo's engine needs no breaking-in period before unleashing the car's huge potential. To ensure that drivers can start wringing the most out of the V10's huge power, the engine is actually run in at the factory before being mounted in the Gallardo.

Lamborghini Gallardo: The Specifications

ENGINE	Aluminium V10	0–125 MPH (0-201 KM/H)	9.0 secs		springs, dampers &
VALVETRAIN	DOHC, 4 valves / cyl	MAXIMUM SPEED	192 mph (309 km/h)		anti-roll bar
	with variable intake	STEERING	Rack and pinion with	SUSPENSION REAR	Double wishbones
	system & continuously		power assist		w/anti-roll bar with coil
	variable valve timing	BRAKES FRONT	Ventilated discs with 8-		springs, dampers &
DISPLACEMENT	4961 cc		piston callipers/		anti-roll bar
MAXIMUM POWER	493 bhp at 7,800 rpm		14 in/365 mm, ABS	CURB WEIGHT	3,373 lbs/1,530 kg
MAXIMUM TORQUE	376 Ib ft at 4,500 rpm	BRAKES REAR	Ventilated discs with 8-	LENGTH	169 in/4,300 mm
TRANSMISSION	Six-speed manual		piston callipers/14 in/	WIDTH	75 in/1,900 mm
	(optional E-gear		335 mm, ABS	HEIGHT	46 in/1,165 mm
	system available)	SUSPENSION FRONT	Double wishbones	WHEELS FRONT	8.5 x 19 in
0–60 MPH (0-100 KM/H)	4.2 secs		w/anti-roll bar with coil	WHEEL REAR	11 x 19 in

Maserati MC12

The car you're looking at is a Ferrari Enzo.
Well, it isn't. But it is. Let us explain...

Up until recently, Maserati was in partnership with Ferrari and thanks to the Italian stallion, the MC12 has its engineering roots in the legendary Ferrari Enzo. It

features the same carbon monocoque, the same V12 engine (albeit detuned), and even the same basic steering wheel and windshield. But the MC12 is aerodynamically superior to the prancing horse. After all, it's 24 inches (610 mm) longer and it features extended overhangs at both the back and rear. That means the engineers have been able to optimize how the air flows over (and exits) the MC12's body.

While the MC12 available to the public isn't the actual car that will race round tracks scooping up awards, it's close enough. Hit the accelerator and any illusions of being in a user-friendly runabout vanish quicker than the car hitting 0–60 mph (0-100 km/h) in 3.8 secs. The MC12 boasts an even power delivery so the driver is constantly pinned back in his racing seat as the car thunders its way up to 205 mph (330 km/h).

The interior of the MC12 is an elegant but functional cockpit with lightweight carbon fiber used in abundance. The carbon fiber seats feature full harnesses, and a large rev counter dominates the MC12's dials.

What's incredible about this supercar is what Masearti managed to achieve in 12 months – it's nothing short of a miracle.

"*The Maserati
MC12 has its
engineering roots
in the legendary
Ferrari Enzo.*"

Long Time Coming

Maserati, a name synonymous with racing excellence, achieved its last victory way back in 1967 with the Cooper Maserati F1 at the South African Grand Prix.

Design Guru

While the MC12 was built for functionality rather than creative form, the supercar still has the kind of road presence that shames many of its competitors – it was designed by Frank Stephenson whose last job before joining up with the Ferrari Maserati Group was to design the Mini Cooper.

What's In A Color?

The MC12 is available only in a two-tone white and blue livery. This color scheme is in homage to the Maserati Tipo 60–61 "Birdcages" from the early 1960s.

Keeping Up With The Joneses

The MC12 is surely the last word in exclusivity – only 50 will ever be made.

Hooked On Air

Like a true Le Mans racer, the MC12 features a large snorkel on its roof and rear grille to shove air down on to the Ferrari Enzo-sourced V12 engine.

Speedy Production

It's claimed that to get the MC12 from the drawing board to the finished car took a year. In fact, every element of creating the car was done at light speed – the alloys took a mere 15 days to go from design to the prototype wheel.

Maserati MC12: The Specifications

ENGINE	V12	**BRAKES FRONT**	Cross-drilled & ventilated discs with 6-piston callipers, ABS/15 in/380 mm	**SUSPENSION REAR**	Double wishbones with push-rod links, steel dampers & coil springs
VALVETRAIN	DOHC, 4 valves / cyl				
DISPLACEMENT	5,998 cc				
MAXIMUM POWER	622 bhp at 7,500 rpm	**BRAKES REAR**	Cross-drilled & ventilated discs with 4-piston callipers, ABS/13 in/335 mm	**CURB WEIGHT**	2,943 lbs/1,335 kg
MAXIMUM TORQUE	480 lb ft at 5,500 rpm			**LENGTH**	202 in/5,143 mm
TRANSMISSION	Six-speed sequential manual			**WIDTH**	82 in/2,096 mm
		SUSPENSION FRONT	Double wishbones with push-rod links, steel dampers & coil springs	**HEIGHT**	47 in/1,205 mm
0–60 MPH (0-100 KM/H)	3.8 secs			**WHEELS FRONT**	9 x 19 in
MAXIMUM SPEED	205 mph (330 km/h)			**WHEEL REAR**	13 x 19 in
STEERING	Rack and pinion with power assist				

Mercedes-Benz McLaren SLR

The three-pointed star wanted to make an impact with their first true supercar. Here's how they pulled it off...

Like its forefather, the new SLR pushes out the technological envelope too – a process helped by teaming up with their Formula One partners, McLaren, who are rather well known for producing what is arguably still the greatest supercar of all time – the McLaren F1.

Just look over the long dart-like form of the car and its arrow-shaped nose, and it's not hard to see how the SLR's design elements are clearly inspired by the Formula One Silver Arrows. That full carbon fiber body encases cutting edge mechanics – a hand-assembled supercharged liter V8 engine, producing 626 bhp (and enough torque to beat its chief rival, the Ferrari Enzo) is mounted towards the front of the chassis. Power delivery is borderline insane.

The only chink in the SLR's formidable armor is its ceramic brakes – they've been regularly criticized for their complete lack of feel, leaving the driver having to learn how to use the SLR's electronically regulated braking power – not something that you particularly want to do in a supercar that can hit 0–60 mph (0-100 km/h) in 3.7 secs.

Opening the gull wing doors of the SLR reveals a snug interior - an optional claret-red leather-swathed interior can be ordered, a color arrangement inspired by the 1950s SLR's interior. Electronically adjustable carbon-frame seats, chronometer-style instruments and the use of carbon fiber and aluminium create an environment that should see drivers happily clocking up hundreds of miles in style.

"The new SLR is a classic, managing to straddle the gap between the ferocious performance of a supercar and the luxuries of a GT."

Smooth Operator

Based on Formula One technology, the SLR's underbody is virtually smooth. That coupled with a six-channel diffuser at the rear means that there is minimal drag and more downforce produced when hitting higher speeds. Even the exhausts have been moved to the side to ensure that aerodynamics aren't affected – those sidepipes also pay tribute to those featured on the 1950s SLR.

Sudden Impact

If an SLR driver should find themselves about to go nose first into an immovable object, they can seek solace in the car's long carbon fiber body and front end crash structure, offering the kind of energy absorption in crashes that has saved many lives on the Formula One circuit.

Acronym Explained

During the SLR's heyday in the 1950s, the SLR stood for Sporty Light Racer.

"How do I start this?"

The SLR has the obligatory starter button. Instead of being mounted in the central console, the glowing red starter button is actually located on the end of the gear lever – simply flip back the cover and push down.

Geared For Action

The five-speed auto gearbox sourced from the Mercedes-owned luxury limo, the Maybach, comes with two automatic settings and three manual ones. The manual settings can be accessed via the gear lever or the steering wheel-mounted buttons.

Mercedes-Benz SLR: The Specifications

ENGINE	AMG V8	STEERING	Rack and pinion with power assist	SUSPENSION FRONT	Double wishbones with coil springs & gas dampers
VALVETRAIN	SOHC, 3 valves / cyl				
DISPLACEMENT	5,439 cc	BRAKES FRONT	Fiber reinforced ceramic discs with eight piston callipers, ESP, SBC/ 14.5 in/370 mm		
MAXIMUM POWER	626 bhp at 6,500 rpm			SUSPENSION REAR	Double wishbones with coil springs & gas dampers
MAXIMUM TORQUE	575 lb ft at 3,250– 5,000 rpm				
				CURB WEIGHT	3,898 lbs/1,768 kg
TRANSMISSION	5-Speed Auto with Speedshift System	BRAKES REAR	Fiber reinforced ceramic discs with 4 piston callipers, ESP, SBC/14 in/360 mm	LENGTH	183 in/4,656 mm
				WIDTH	75 in/1,908 mm
0–60 MPH (0-100 KM/H)	3.7 secs			HEIGHT	50 in/1,261 mm
0–125 MPH (0-201 KM/H)	10.7 secs			WHEELS FRONT	9 x 18 in
MAXIMUM SPEED	208 mph (335 km/h)			WHEEL REAR	11.5 x 18 in

Mitsubishi Lancer Evolution VIII 400

Copyright Mitsubishi Motors Ltd

While supercars can trace their DNA back to the race track, the Evo range was born out of the mud, gravel and pot holes of rallying...

The Evo VIII FQ-400 can produce a G-force that would give the sort of Hollywood facelift that an aging actress would kill for. In the 3.5 secs it takes to hit 60 mph

Copyright Mitsubishi Motors Ltd

(97 km/h), the trouble is that it could also age you if you're not up to handling the Evo's huge power.

While the FQ-400 may be easy to handle driving round town at low revs, hit the magic power band at 5,000 rpm, and the turbo kicks in properly. Once the turbo is churning out

its power through the rally-sourced four-wheel drive, you won't be able to believe that it's all coming from a 2-liter turbo-charged engine. This car produces a whopping 405 bhp.

With neutral handling, tidy body control and colossal grip, the Evo can devour corners with unnerving confidence. Many argue though that the FQ-400 is simply too extreme and that FQ-340 version will give you great performance but of the sort that can be used more frequently on the average trip to the supermarket.

Remember that this is a Japanese car so reliability comes as standard – but this extreme engineering of the Evo has the benefit of being backed-up by a three year/ 36,000 miles warranty – that even includes drivers who've taken to tearing their Evos round tracks on a regular basis.

Copyright Mitsubishi Motors Ltd

"*Being a rally car designed for the road, the Evo can do the twisty stuff as well as the 0–100 mph (0-161 km/h) assault on your senses. With neutral handling, tidy body control and colossal grip, the Evo can devour corners with unnerving confidence.*"

Frightfully Quick

The MR stands for "Mitsubishi Racing" but ever wondered what the FQ in the MR FQ-400 stands for?

Number Crunching...

The Pagani Zonda cranks out a very respectable 76.12 bhp per liter. The Porsche Carrera GT manages 106.75. The FQ-400 claims 202.5 bhp per liter.

Need For FQ Speed

The FQ-400 is not only the fastest road car that Mitsubishi has ever made (for the UK market at least) – it also has the honor of being the fastest accelerating four-door sedan, from a major manufacturer, ever to grace public roads.

Ready To Launch

To keep the FQ-400's immense power welded to the road, instead of coming off at the first corner, Mitsubishi's engineers have made sure that the car remains stable at high speeds with the inclusion of a carbon fiber front lip spoiler, Ralliart aero mirrors and the rather menacing rear vortex generator – the "shark's teeth" that can be found poking out of the rear of the roof.

So Little, So Much

Just how did Mitsubishi manage to get so much brake horse power out of a 2-liter engine? The most important element is the Garrett turbocharger made especially for the FQ-400, and the engine has also been strengthened to withstand the huge forces needed to develop 405 bhp.

Mitsubishi Lancer Evo VIII MR FQ-400: The Specifications

ENGINE	Inline-4	**BRAKES FRONT**	Alcon 6-pot monobloc brake kit/13 in/343 mm	**SUSPENSION REAR**	McPherson strut suspension with inverted shock absorbers, stabilizer bar & aluminium front lower arms
VALVETRAIN	DOHC turbo with intercooler	**BRAKES REAR**	Ventilated discs with 2-pot aluminium callipers/12 in/300 mm		
DISPLACEMENT	1,997 cc				
MAXIMUM POWER	405 bhp at 6,400 rpm	**SUSPENSION FRONT**	McPherson strut suspension with inverted shock absorbers, stabilizer bar & aluminium front lower arms	**CURB WEIGHT**	3,086 lbs/1,400 kg
MAXIMUM TORQUE	355 lb ft at 5,500 rpm			**LENGTH**	177 in/4,490 mm
TRANSMISSION	Six-speed manual			**WIDTH**	70 in/1,770 mm
0–60 MPH(0-100 KM/H)	3.5 secs			**HEIGHT**	57 in/1,450 mm
0–100 MPH(0-161 KM/H)	9.1 secs			**WHEELS FRONT**	8 x 17 in
MAXIMUM SPEED	175 mph (282 km/h)			**WHEEL REAR**	8 x 17 in
STEERING	Rack and pinion with power assist				

Pagani Zonda

Exotic, outlandish, eccentric... the Zonda is the most individual supercar the world has ever seen...

First revealed at the Geneva Motor Show, Switzerland, in 1999, the prototype of the Zonda was always going to cause a fuss – with those alien looks, it simply couldn't fail not to. At the heart of the car is its unique use of composite materials with a carbon fiber chassis and body, ensuring an incredibly lightweight and rigid structure. Add into that a bullet-proof, smooth-revving Mercedes-Benz AMG V12 – after all, those Germans know how to build a reliable engine that won't blow up when you're attempting to top 200 mph (322 km/h). The original five-speed C12 had 389 bhp on tap in 6.9-liter form and has been constantly evolving ever since. The six-speed Zonda C12 S which is shown here has now evolved into the S 7.3 – all 555 bhp of it boasting a 0–60 mph (0-100 km/h) time of 3.6 secs. Traction control is included, which is mighty handy for nailing all that power to the road in wet conditions.

Perhaps the most keenly anticipated Pagani was the 555 bhp Roadster – but there was a genuine concern among fans that chopping off the roof of the Zonda would leave its handling horribly compromised. But again, Pagani and his team managed to blow away any concerns by introducing a new carbon fiber central chassis structure, and a roll bar made from carbon and chrome-molybdene to ensure that rigidity remained at the heart of the Zonda Roadster's winning formula.

The most extreme Zonda was introduced in 2005 – the F version. Built alongside the standard Zonda, it features a lighter chassis and better aerodynamics courtesy of a host of changes including a larger front splitter. That monster Mercedes engine is now even more powerful thanks to a new induction system which means you've got a whopping 602 bhp under your right foot – the power-hungry driver wanting even more acceleration can of course settle for the Clubsport edition that boasts 650 bhp.

"The Zonda was always going to cause a fuss. With those alien looks, it simply couldn't fail not to."

Exclusivity Guaranteed

The Roadster is regarded as the most desirable of the Zonda range. Roadster's production will be capped at only 40.

What's In A Name?

What's a supercar without a suitably evocative name? The word Zonda actually comes from a warm wind that blows west across the Andes Mountains in South America.

In Good Company

The Zonda's creator Horacio Pagani had expert help from the now-deceased Grand Prix racing legend, Juan Manuel Fangio. He is credited with aiding Horacio with all aspects of the supercar's creation – from its styling to its world-class handling.

Bespoke Heaven

The interior of the Zonda is as unique as its exterior with its mix of aluminium, leather and carbon fiber. Of course, for that special supercar touch, the company also provides owners with bespoke leather luggage and a pair of driving shoes with every car.

Leap Of Faith

Talk about conviction – Horacio Pagani was so sure that the Zonda would be a hit with the public once they'd seen it at the 1999 Geneva Motor Show, that he'd already had the car crash tested and ramped up ready for production.

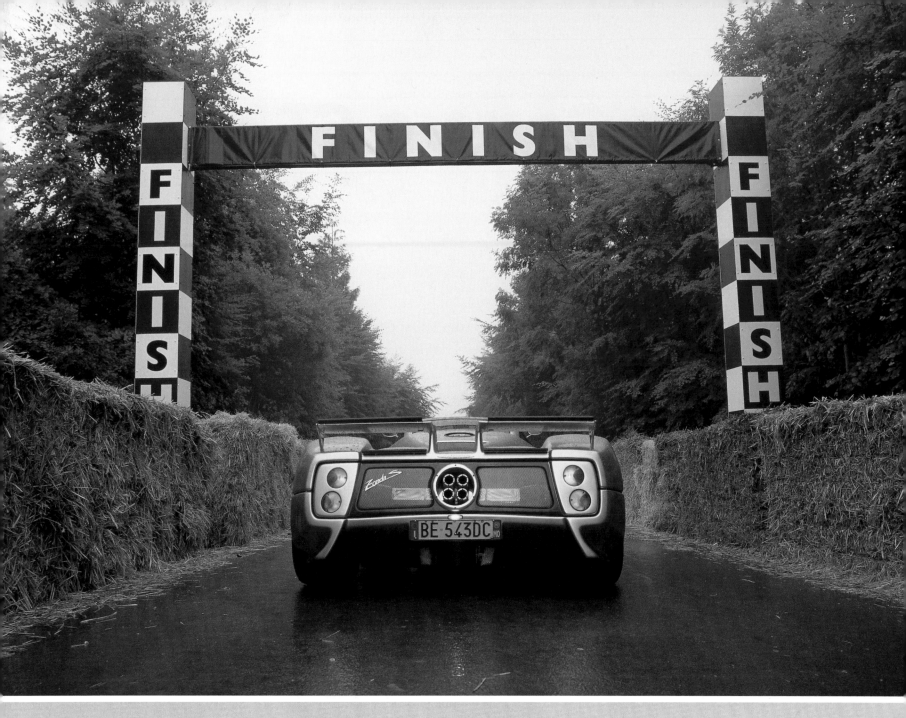

Pagani Zonda S 7.3: The Specifications

ENGINE	V12	STEERING	Rack and pinion with power assist	SUSPENSION REAR	Double wishbones with helical springs, hydraulic dampers & anti-roll bar
VALVETRAIN	DOHC 4 valves / cyl				
DISPLACEMENT	7,291 cc	BRAKES FRONT	Ventilated with four-piston callipers, ABS/14 in/355 mm		
MAXIMUM POWER	555 bhp at 5,900 rpm			CURB WEIGHT	2,976 lbs/1,350 kg
MAXIMUM TORQUE	553 lb ft at 4,050 rpm	BRAKES REAR	Ventilated with four-piston callipers, ABS/14 in/355 mm	LENGTH	173 in/4,395 mm
TRANSMISSION	Six-speed manual			WIDTH	81 in/2,055 mm
0–60 MPH (0-100 KM/H)	3.6 secs	SUSPENSION FRONT	Double wishbones with helical springs, hydraulic dampers & anti-roll bar	HEIGHT	45 in/1,151 mm
0–100 MPH (0-161 KM/H)	Sub 8 secs			WHEELS FRONT	9 x 18 in
MAXIMUM SPEED	220 mph (354 km/h)			WHEEL REAR	13 x 18 in

Porsche Carrera GT

Sports car maker Porsche had been out of the supercar game for decades. Trust them to come storming back onto the scene with a road racer that makes all the right noises...

It's been a long while coming – the last time Porsche unleashed anything resembling a true supercar on to the world stage was with the magnificent 959 back in 1987.

The GT's racing heritage is apparent throughout the car – it's got Formula One-style all-wishbone pushrod suspension, a brand new V10 engine (that was initially bound for Le Mans), and a small ceramic clutch that's mated to a six-speed manual transmission. Thanks to that diminutive clutch, it means the engine can be mounted lower in the car; the end result being better weight distribution and aerodynamics.

Unlike the normally rear-engined Porsches, the V10 is mounted in the middle and produces 612 bhp. The low-weight carbon fiber monocoque chassis coupled with such power means that the GT can do the 0–60 mph (0–100 km/h) sprint in 3.8 secs and 0–100 (0–161 km/h)in a mere 6.9 secs.

City driving needn't be a handful either with the car willing to idle along before you decide to floor the accelerator and be pushed back into the seat with its startling but ultimately progressive grunt – there are no nasty surprises awaiting the keen, experienced driver.

No one should be surprised that Porsche has managed to pull off a masterstroke with their supercar entry – the GT shows just what we've all been missing out on while Porsche has been in supercar hibernation. It's just a shame it took them so long to rejoin the party. Welcome back, Porsche – we've missed you.

"On the twisty stuff, the GT comes into its own offering a benign drive that is all about feel and communication coupled with huge grip."

119

Touching Wood

A Porsche with a wood gear knob? It may seem out of place in a car that uses the latest composite materials, but that gear knob is a nod to the 1970–1971 Le Mans champ, the Porsche 917. So, why wood in the 917? Because it was the lightest material of that time – and it stopped the driver from scalding his hand when shifting gears.

Suited And Booted

There is space under the front hood for luggage in the GT but don't expect to be able to pack any kind of suitcase in there. In the meantime, Porsche provides a specially tailored travel bag to fit into the limited space.

Wheely, Wheely Good

To make a supercar, you have to be weight-obsessed – and Porsche is the "supermodel" of supercars. For example, unlike most supercars that use aluminium alloy for their wheels, Porsche has used lighter forged magnesium. And those wheels need to be as light as possible – after all, they measure 19 in at the front and a whopping 20 in at the rear.

Perfect Service

Porsche claim that the GT requires the engine oil and air filter to be changed only every 12,000 miles; the oil filter every 24,000 miles; and the spark plugs every four years or 24,000 miles.

Porsche Carrera GT: The Specifications

ENGINE	Aluminium V10	BRAKES FRONT	Porsche Ceramic Composite Brake (PCCB). Ventilated and cross-drilled with six-piston callipers, ABS/15 in/380 mm	SUSPENSION REAR	Double wishbones with inboard springs inc. dampers units
VALVETRAIN	DOHC 4 valves / cyl				
DISPLACEMENT	5,733 cc				
MAXIMUM POWER	612 bhp at 8,000 rpm			CURB WEIGHT	3,042 lbs/1,380 kg
MAXIMUM TORQUE	435 lb ft at 5,750 rpm			LENGTH	182 in/4,613 mm
TRANSMISSION	Six-speed manual with two-plate ceramic dry clutch	BRAKES REAR	Porsche Ceramic Composite Brake (PCCB). Ventilated and cross-drilled with six-piston callipers, ABS/15 in/380 mm	WIDTH	76 in/1,921 mm
				HEIGHT	46 in/1,166 mm
				WHEELS FRONT	9.5 x 19 in
0–60 MPH (0-100 KM/H)	3.8 secs			WHEEL REAR	12.5 x 20 in
0–100 MPH (0-161 KM/H)	6.9 secs				
MAXIMUM SPEED	205 mph (330 km/h)	SUSPENSION FRONT	Double wishbones with inboard springs inc. dampers units		
STEERING	Rack and pinion with power assist				

TVR Sagaris

It's loud; it's rude; it's not one for small talk, and it doesn't want to be everyone's friend... it's a TVR then...

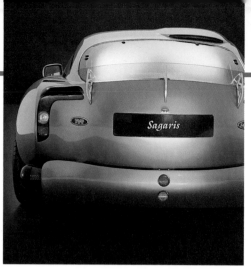

Look over the composite GRP bodywork of the TVR and your senses are assaulted from every angle – those dragon-esque headlamps, the mass of hood vents; and on the car's rear, well, have you ever seen a transparent rear spoiler? No, we thought not. Underneath, there's typical TVR firepower on offer for the brave-hearted driver. The Sagaris was intended to be a trackday car born out of the pretty TVR T350 that would also be suitable for road

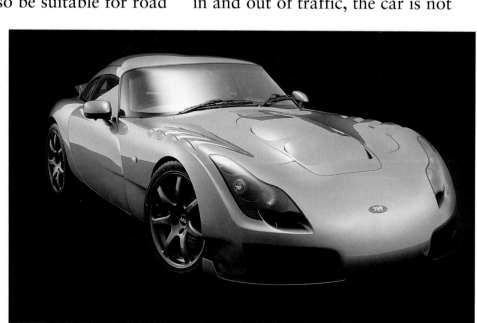

use; and with the finished car now bedazzling drivers, TVR has delivered on that promise.

With its 0-60 mph (0–100 km/h) time of 3.7 secs and 0-100 mph (0–161 km/h) in 8.1 secs, the 400 bhp 4-liter engine mounted on the Sagaris's tubular steel chassis is easy to exploit with its five-speed gearbox. But for all its obvious drama, the Sagaris is day-to-day useable. While threading in and out of traffic, the car is not

trying to scrabble to get away from you; however, show it the right road, and the Sagaris demonstrates its true TVR roots. Of course it's very quick with huge grip.

Inside the Sagaris is equally special – two white dials peer out at the driver from the dashboard while the rest of the cabin is smothered in leather. Everything on view is bespoke – apart from the three-spoke steering wheel. You'll also notice the roll cage, there to reassure anyone that while the car lacks electronic safety devices, you'll be well looked after if the worst does happen.

With its unmatched charisma, no-nonsense approach and obscene performance, the low volume British TVR range is something to be cherished.

"Visually, TVR doesn't do subtle, and the Sagaris is like being poked in the eye with an electric cattle prod. It's that shocking; it makes supercars such as the Ferrari F430 look everyday and hum-drum."

A Brief (Recent) History Of TVR

TVR was founded in 1947 – but in 2004, the company was sold to a 24-year-old wealthy entrepreneur, Nikolai Smolenski. His initial moves to take TVR into the 21st century have been to address the build quality issues that have plagued the handmade TVRs of the past; because customers have been put off by reliability issues, the Russian delayed the release of the Sagaris and the Tuscan 2 to ensure that build quality was improved.

Bound For The US?

While TVR has amassed a cult following in the US thanks to games such as the *Gran Turismo* series and movies like *Swordfish*, the car isn't available to the US public. Only time will tell if the new owner of TVR has plans to unleash the brand in America.

"I'm A TV-R Star"

The Sagaris prototype unveiled to thrilled audiences in 2003 went on to become one of the stars of British reality TV show *The Heist* where ex-criminals were charged with the task of stealing it. They succeeded.

Keeping It Close

The factory in Blackpool, England, makes practically everything you see inside and outside of a TVR, and the company's straight-six engines are the stuff of motoring legend.

Sagaris: The Specifications

ENGINE	All-aluminium TVR Speed Six straight-six	**STEERING**	Rack and pinion with power assist	**SUSPENSION REAR**	Independent double wishbones with coils over gas hydraulic dampers & anti-roll bar
DISPLACEMENT	3,996 cc	**BRAKES FRONT**	Ventilated discs with 4-piston alloy callipers/ 13 in/322 mm		
MAXIMUM POWER	406 bhp at 7,000-7,500 bhp				
				CURB WEIGHT	2,376 lbs/1,078 kg
MAXIMUM TORQUE	349 lb ft at 5,000 rpm	**BRAKES REAR**	Ventilated discs with single sliding piston callipers/12 in/298 mm	**LENGTH**	160 in/4,057 mm
TRANSMISSION	Five-speed manual			**WIDTH**	73 in/1,850 mm
MPH (0-100 KM/H)	3.7 secs			**HEIGHT**	46 in/1,175 mm
MPH (0-161 KM/H)	8.1 secs	**SUSPENSION FRONT**	Independent double wishbones with coils over gas hydraulic dampers & anti-roll bar		
MAXIMUM SPEED	175 mph (282 km/h)				

TVR Tuscan 2

Now in its second generation, the Tuscan has grown up to become a more civilized supercar than the youthful original. But the beast still lurks beneath those strikingly beautiful looks...

Featuring TVR's incredible straight-six engine that produces a whopping 350 bhp, the Tuscan 2 is blindingly fast – 0-60 mph (0-100 km/h) takes 4.2 secs, and the supercar will happily see 175 mph (282 km/h) and beyond. But TVR's engineers aren't known for sitting back and slapping themselves on the back for a job well down; they've been busy tinkering and have produced the top of the range Tuscan 2 S that features 400 bhp on tap and can hit 0-60 mph (0-100 km/h) in 3.8 secs – goodbye Gallardo. All that power is kept on the road at high speed thanks to a splitter under the front grille and a gurney above the hood lid that ensures downforce over both the front and rear axles.

Climb inside the TVR and the sight of a fully bespoke interior will greet you; all the vital readouts such as speed and revs are digital; the leather upholstery is made by TVR in-house, and the alloy switchgear is tactile and satisfying to use. There is an issue though for anyone familiar with the TVR brand – build quality.

The development of the TVR Tuscan 2 and the Sagaris though saw them being put through punishing conditions in Bahrain, South Africa, Saudi Arabia and Russia for the first time to ensure that the car could take high speeds in gruelling environments. Whether all the "gremlins" have been wiped out remains to be seen though – only time will tell but with its three year/36,000 mile warranty, TVR is backing up its new found commitment to build quality with its bank balance.

"Driving a TVR on the limit requires focus and concentration, and there's precious little safety equipment on board if it all starts to go pear-shaped – no traction control, no ABS, no, well, anything – just an integrated roll-cage. The Tuscan's no pussycat but no TVR ever should be."

Doing It Differently

TVR is known for not playing by the rules with any element of its cars. They even have to do their doors differently – don't go looking for a traditional handle by the way; pushing a button underneath the wing mirror makes the window slip down, the door gently springing open. Now how's that for bespoke?

Bark Worse Than Its Bite?

The TVR's straight-six engine sounds incredible – the deep roar that bellows every time you floor the car is a marvel – but the original Tuscan could bite in the handling department. The Tuscan 2 features a revised geometry, improved bump stops plus re-rated springs and dampers so that the car can be manhandled more easily when pushing the Tuscan 2 to its limits. But still, it's advised that the TVR is handled with care.

Practical As Well As Powerful

Many supercars require you to shoe-horn any luggage into them using either bespoke bags... or a crowbar. The Tuscan 2 however can happily take two golf bags, which means the car's actually practical as well as sensational.

Lighten Up

The key to the Tuscan 2's searing performance is the fact that it weighs so little – with a curb weight of only 2,425 lbs (1,100 kg) to cart around, that 4-liter straight-six engine can offer supercar performance without the need for added extras.

134

TVR Tuscan 2: The Specifications

ENGINE	All-aluminium TVR Speed Six straight-six	BRAKES FRONT	Ventilated discs with 4-piston alloy callipers/ 12 in/304 mm	SUSPENSION REAR	Independent double wish bones with coils over gas hydraulic dampers & anti-roll bar
DISPLACEMENT	3,605 cc				
MAXIMUM POWER	350 bhp at 7,200 rpm	BRAKES REAR	Ventilated discs with single sliding piston calipers/11 in/282 mm	CURB WEIGHT	2,425 lbs/1,100 kg
MAXIMUM TORQUE	290 lb ft at 5,500 rpm			LENGTH	167 in/4,235 mm
TRANSMISSION	Five-speed manual			WIDTH	71 in/1,810 mm
0–60 MPH (0-100 KM/H)	4.2 secs	SUSPENSION FRONT	Independent double wish bones with coils over gas hydraulic dampers & anti-roll bar	HEIGHT	47 in/1,200 mm
0–100 MPH (0-161 KM/H)	9.5 secs			WHEELS FRONT	8 x 16 in
MAXIMUM SPEED	175 mph (282 km/h)			WHEEL REAR	8 x 16 in
STEERING	Rack and pinion with power assist				

Future Perfect?

It seems like we've hit perfection with the supercar. So where do you go from here? How do you top what seems insurmountable? Well, judging from the various developments and news (and a fair smattering of rumors too), the best is inevitability still to come. The supercar community's desire to outdo each other and seduce buyers will see the arrival of more potential supercar classics over the next few years.

For example, McLaren re-entered the scene aproper in 2008 with its supercar codenamed the P8. Featuring a Mercedes-sourced 6.3-liter V8, the P8 is able to produce above 500 bhp and over 440 lb ft of torque.

Then there are the left-of-the-middle entries such as Project 1221's MF1. Details are scant about this emerging supercar but the makers claim it will have unmatched handling and agility plus a large luggage capacity. Yes, you may have heard such hyperbole a dozen times before but the MF1 could actually deliver. After all, it's being engineered by the former technical director of Lamborghini and Bugatti, Mauro Forghieri.

As for the far future, there's that 300 mph (483 km/h) barrier to break, and it has been predicted that supercars will produce in excess of 2,000 bhp, weigh 25 percent less than current crop and could even hit 350 mph(563 km/h). Sounds like the ramblings of the mad but there is a supercar that's set to touch down that could potentially leave the outrageous performance of current supercars for dead, and offer an enticing and very real glimpse of what the future of the supercar has in store for us...

Enter the Bugatti Veyron.

Bugatti Veyron

Fact or fiction? The latest legend to bear the Bugatti name could finally be with us after a very long development period...

Copyright Bugatti Automobiles S.A.S.

Death in the Bugatti family; a failed revival; and a rebirth followed by a humiliating bankruptcy when the world sank into recession in the 1990s – reading Bugatti's history, you could be forgiven for thinking that the company is cursed. Even in the hands of Volkswagen, the development of the latest car to bear the Bugatti name – the Veyron – was at one point halted. But now VW has the car back on track with delivery of the first Veyron to one lucky (and rich) customer at the end of 2005.

Any supercar fan knows why it's essential that the Veyron does finally touch down – after all, it could potentially rip asunder every supercar that's gone before it. Here are the figures – it's got nearly 1,000 bhp on tap; it's got not one, but 4 turbos; it's expected to weigh in at just under 2.2 tons; it can go from 0–60 mph (0-100 km/h) in an estimated 3 secs; it has a potentially record-breaking top speed of over 250 mph (402 km/h); it features the biggest rear tires ever fitted on a production car; it has four wheel drive of course. In fact, everything about this supercar is big – the DSG gearbox even has 7 gears to make the most of (and more importantly, tame) the Veyron's amazing W16, 64v quad-turbo 8-liter engine.

Copyright Bugatti Automobiles S.A.S.

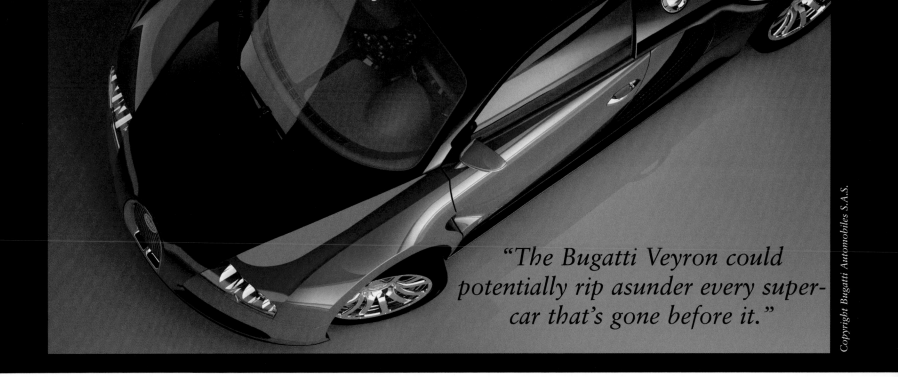

"The Bugatti Veyron could potentially rip asunder every super-car that's gone before it."

Tall Order?

Volkswagen intends to make between 30 to 50 Veyrons a year depending on the demand from customers. And if you're wondering if Volkswagen is actually up to the job of selling supercars, bear in mind that they own Audi – the company that oversaw the creation of the next generation of Lamborghinis.

Back To Its Roots

The Veyron is being assembled at a workshop right next to Chateau St Jean near Molsheim in France – which is the region where the company's founder, Ettore Bugatti, began making his dream cars nearly 100 years ago.

Brake Neck Speeds

With nearly 1,000 bhp to propel the driver towards the horizon, it's fairly important that the Veyron can stop as quickly as it can start. To aid in avoiding near disaster when a car pulls out in front of you while you're doing 200 mph+ (322 km/h) on a German autobahn, the Veyron is fitted with specialist carbon-ceramic brakes and a rear wing that can be deployed as an air brake. It is claimed that slamming on the brakes at 248 mph (399 km/h)will bring the Veyron to a complete standstill in less than 10secs.

Bugatti Veyron (specifications subject to change)

ENGINE	64v quad turbo W16	TRANSMISSION	Seven-speed DSG	HEIGHT	47 in/1,206 mm
VALVETRAIN	DOHC 4 Valves / Cyl	0–60 MPH (0-100 KM/H)	3.0 secs	WHEELS FRONT	9.5 x 20 in
DISPLACEMENT	7,993 cc	MAXIMUM SPEED	252 mph (406 km/h)	WHEEL REAR	13 x 21 in
MAXIMUM POWER	987 bhp at 6,000 rpm	CURB WEIGHT	4,299 lbs/1,950 kg approx.		
MAXIMUM TORQUE	922 lb ft at 2,200-5,500 rpm	LENGTH	172 in/4,380 mm		
		WIDTH	78 in/1,994 mm		

Supercars on a Budget

Save winning the lottery, it's inevitable that the intoxicating delights of owning a Lamborghini or a Pagani are well out of the reach of most us; for now, at least. But there's no reason to despair (or seriously consider a career in armed robbery) because there are cars out there that can offer similar thrills to the supercar, but for a fraction of the price.

We're featuring four candidates for your deliberation here that cover a lot of the supercar bases such as great (or outlandish) looks, thrilling performances and handling that delights at every corner. And if none of these suit your budget, take solace in the fact that a quick flick through those local classifieds for secondhand cars will reveal some real driving gems. Think Mazda RX-7 or Subaru Impreza Turbo to name but two of the classics available that guarantee maximum fun for minimal money. After all, there's something for everybody to live out those driving dreams. We'll see you on the road...

Ariel Atom 2

No, it's not your typical looking supercar but hey, the British aren't known for settling for the same old, same old...

Perhaps the Atom is the antithesis to the supercar scene's sometimes seriousness. With no swish bodywork covering up its ultra-lightweight chassis, everything is out on display. Perhaps this is a road car that can truly be said to be a perfect example of form following function. And the great thing about the Atom is that its function is so simple – to make you remember why you fell in love with driving in the first place.

The car's unique composite twin seat unit means that you won't find yourself (or your passenger) being thrown all over the cockpit. Well, it's hardly even a cockpit – there are no frills here, merely the basics required to get started.

As for the Atom's performance on the straight stuff, you can see why the car has gone down a storm – the Ariel Atom 2 released in 2003 offers up the perfect performance to help induce

that feel-good factor – after all, it features one of world's finest budget engines (and six-speed gearboxes) whipped straight out of a Japanese-spec Honda Civic Type R, which produces 220 bhp. But bear in mind that the Atom weighs only 1,005 lbs (456 kg) – with such a lean curb weight, it makes the likes of Zonda and Enzo look in need of a two-week diet. And just to rub the salt into those supercar wounds, Ariel offers the Atom in an "enhanced" supercharged version boasting an insane 300 bhp. Helmet recommended.

"The Ariel Atom 2 features one of the world's finest budget engines whipped straight out of a Japanese-spec Honda Civic Type R."

Ariel Atom 2: The Specifications

ENGINE	Honda iVTEC / 4 Cyl	MAXIMUM TORQUE	145 lb ft at 6,100 rpm	MAXIMUM SPEED	135 mph (217 km/h)
DISPLACEMENT	1,998 cc	TRANSMISSION	Six-speed manual	CURB WEIGHT	1,025 lbs (456 kg)
MAXIMUM POWER	220 bhp at 8,200 rpm	0–60 MPH (0-100 KM/H)	3.5 secs		

Lotus Exige

Offering outstanding performance on the track, and the ability to be an everyday runabout, the Exige is also packed with racing pedigree...

The miracle makers based in Norfolk, UK, first launched the Lotus Exige in 2000; the mid-engine coupe was actually based on the Mk I Lotus Elise, the firm's critically acclaimed two-seater roadster. In 2004 though, the Exige was relaunched this time featuring a Toyota 1.8-liter VVT-i engine instead of the original's Rover K-series. The bullet-proof Toyota engine generates 189 bhp, which makes the Exige zip from 0–60 mph (0–100 km/h) in 4.9 secs. The Exige's underpinnings are now based on the Elise Mk II – in fact, the extruded and bonded aluminium tub, with a steel rear subframe, is used in the Elise 111R.

The specially commissioned Lotus Exige Sport features carbon fiber bodywork and front splitter, a rear diffuser, and an adjustable rear wing for added downforce. Instead of the Toyota engine, there's a 400 bhp 3-liter V6 lump paired with a sequential six-speed gearbox.

Customers wanting a more extreme version of the standard Exige will have to make do with Exige Sport 240R, which features 240 hp and a supercar-crushing 0–60 mph (0–100 km/h) in 3.9 secs – do bear in mind though that only 50 will ever see the light of day. So best to get that order in now.

"*No corner is too sharp or scary for the Exige. The question isn't whether the car can take it; the real question is can you?*"

Lotus Exige:
The Specifications

ENGINE	Aluminium Inline-4
DISPLACEMENT	1,796 cc
MAXIMUM POWER	189 bhp at 7,800 rpm
MAXIMUM TORQUE	133.5 lb ft at 6,800 rpm
TRANSMISSION	Six-speed manual
0-60 MPH (0-100 KM/H)	4.9 secs
0-100 MPH (0-161 KM/H)	13.2 secs
MAXIMUM SPEED	147 mph (237 km/h)
CURB WEIGHT	1,929 lbs/875 kg

Mercedes-Benz SLK350

Luxury and performance all wrapped up in mini-supercar looks. The SLK350 is one very special car...

The original SLK was a great car – for non-enthusiasts. Its main party trick was the ability to turn from a coupe into an open-top roadster in seconds thanks to its smart metal retractable roof. The trouble was, for all its sporty pretensions, it could never match the might of the sublime Porsche Boxster. Enter the SLK MkII.

It's those looks – the original SLK may have been a smart if slightly effeminate design, but the SLK MkII is far more like a muscular roadster thanks to its F1-style nose inspired by its (very) big brother, the SLR. The folding metal roof remains and is now more of an elegant design – and more importantly, it goes up quickly in case rain interrupts play.

The entry model SLK200 powered by a supercharged 1.8-liter is best suited to those who want more show than go. It provides adequate performance for a droptop – 0-60mph (0–100 km/h) in 8.3 secs – but hardly the kind of acceleration that will trouble a sporty family sedan, never mind a full-blooded supercar with a V12. No, the model to aim for is the rather fine SLK350. Featuring a warbling 3.5-liter V6, the torque-happy engine offers plenty of power for the thrill seeker.

The SLK also now has a quality six-speed gearbox as standard for the driver who likes to feel absolutely in control of that V6 in front of him. Mercedes claims that the auto shaves 0.1 secs off the 0–60 mph (0–100 km/h) time. Whether it shaves some of the fun off too is open to debate.

"The SLK350 is a near-perfect blend; a bruiser when you're in the mood and an extremely comfortable cruiser when you're not".

Mercedes-Benz SLK350: The Specifications

ENGINE	V6
DISPLACEMENT	3,498 cc
MAXIMUM POWER	272 bhp at 6,000 rpm
MAXIMUM TORQUE	258 lb ft at 2,400 rpm
TRANSMISSION	Six-speed manual/ Seven-speed auto
0-60 MPH (0-100 KM/H)	5.6 secs
MAXIMUM SPEED	155 mph (249 km/h)
CURB WEIGHT	3,231 lbs/1,465 kg

Vauxhall VX220 Turbo

Supercar performance, but at a fraction of the price. Discover the small car guaranteed to deliver big grins...

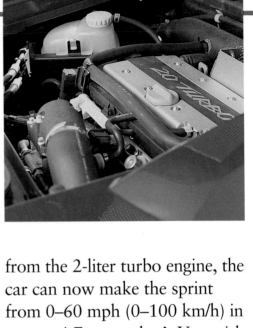

Welcome to the rather brilliant Vauxhall VX220 Turbo. It's all the more remarkable if you consider the car's manufacturer – Vauxhall (owned by General Motors), in the UK, has been perceived for decades as a rather run-of-the-mill car manufacturer.

So creating excitement became the job of the original VX220 launched in 2000. On the face of it, Vauxhall should have struggled to produce such a fantastic two-seater roadster but they had help – they went to Lotus.

Featuring an aluminium chassis and plastic body panels, the original VX220 had a 2.2-liter engine that could do 0-60 mph (0–100 km/h) in 5.6 secs. But that wasn't powerful enough for Vauxhall... so they released the VX220 Turbo. Featuring 197 bhp from the 2-liter turbo engine, the car can now make the sprint from 0–60 mph (0–100 km/h) in a mere 4.7 secs – that's Vanquish S country – and it has a top speed of 151 mph (243 km/h), which is more than enough for a public road. The handling of the VX is superb as well – flat and taut with large dollops of information being fed back to the driver about what is going on under the tires. This may be a serious driver's car, but treat it with the respect it deserves, and it's also real controllable fun.

In 2004, Vauxhall released an even hotter version of the VX, the VXR220, which could hit 0–60 mph (0–100 km/h) in only 4.2 secs and only ran out of puff at 154 mph (248 km/h). Alas, due to its limited production number of 65 cars, they all sold out in six weeks – typical supercar then.

"Vauxhall should have struggled to produce such a fantastic two-seater roadster but they had help... they went to Lotus."

Vauxhall VX220 Turbo: The Specifications

ENGINE	Inline-4
DISPLACEMENT	1,998 cc
MAXIMUM POWER	197 bhp at 5,500 rpm
MAXIMUM TORQUE	184 lb ft from 1,950 rpm
TRANSMISSION	Six-speed manual
0-60 MPH (0-100 KM/H)	4.7 secs
0-100 MPH (0-161 KM/H)	Under 13 secs
MAXIMUM SPEED	151 mph (243 km/h)
CURB WEIGHT	2,050 lbs/930 kg

159

Supercars Comparison Chart

Model	Maximum Power	0-60 (sec)	mph / km/h	Weight (lbs/kg)	Length (in/mm)
Mercedes 3005L Gullwing	240 bhp at 6,100 rpm	8.8	135 / 216	N/A	N/A
Ford GT40 MkIII	306 bhp at 6,000 rpm	5.5	170 / 272	N/A	N/A
Lamborghini Muira	385 bhp at 7,850 rpm	6	180 / 288	N/A	N/A
Lamborghini Countach	375 bhp at 8,000 rpm	5.6	180 / 288	N/A	N/A
BMW M1	277 bhp at 6,500 rpm	5.6	162 / 259.2	N/A	N/A
Lotus Turbo Esprit	210 bhp at 6,250 rpm	5.6	150 / 240	N/A	N/A
Ferrari 288 GTO	390 bhp at 6,300 rpm	5.6	180 / 288	N/A	N/A
Ferrari Testarossa	390 bhp at 6,300 rpm	5.3	180 / 288	N/A	N/A
Porsche 959	450 bhp at 6,500 rpm	3.6	197 / 315.2	N/A	N/A
Ferrari F40	450 bhp at 6,500 rpm	3.6	197 / 315.2	N/A	N/A
Bugatti EB110	603 bhp at 8,250 rpm	3.1	218 / 348.8	N/A	N/A
Jaguar XJ220	542 bhp at 6,500 rpm	3.6	210 / 336	N/A	N/A
McLaren F1	627 bhp at 7,400 rpm	3.2	240 / 384	N/A	N/A
Ferrari F50	513 bhp at 8,000 rpm	3.7	202 / 323.2	N/A	N/A
Aston Martin Vanquish S	520 bhp at 7,000 rpm	4.7	200 / 320	4,134 lbs / 1,875 kg	184 in / 4,665 mm
Aston Martin DBS	450 bhp at 6,000 rpm	4.7	186 / 297.6	3,968 lbs / 1,800 kg	185 in / 4,710 mm
Aston Martin VB Vantage	380 bhp at 7,000 rpm	4.8	175 / 280	3,461 lbs / 1,570 kg	173 in / 4,383 mm
B Engineering Edonis	720 bhp at 8,000 rpm	4	223 / 356.8	3,307 lbs / 1,500 kg	171 in / 4,350 mm

Model	Maximum Power	0-60 (sec)	mph / km/h	Weight (lbs/kg)	Length (in/mm)
Ferarri Enzo	660 bhp at 7,800 rpm	3.5	217 / 347.2	3,009 lbs / 1,365 kg	185 in / 4,702 mm
Ferrari F430	483 bhp at 8,500 rpm	4	196 / 313.6	3,197 lbs / 1,450 kg	178 in / 4,512 mm
Ford GT	483 bhp at 8.500 rpm	4	196 / 313.6	3,197 lbs / 1,450 kg	178 in / 4,512 mm
Honda NSX Coupe 3.2 VB	276 bhp at 7,300 rpm	4.9	168 / 268.8	3,968 lbs / 1,800 kg	174 in / 4,430 mm
Koenigsegg CCR	806 bhp at 6,900 rpm	5.9	242 / 387.2	2,711 lbs / 1,230 kg	164 in / 4,190 mm
Lamborghini Murcielago	580 bhp at 7,500 rpm	3.8	205 / 328	3,638 lbs / 1,650 kg	180 in / 4,580 mm
Lamborghini Gallardo	493 bhp at 7.800 rpm	4.2	192 / 307.2	3,373 lbs / 1,530 kg	169 in / 4,300 mm
Maserati MC12	622 bhp at 7,500 rpm	3.8	205 / 328	2,943 lbs / 1,335 kg	202 in / 5,143 mm
Mercedes-Benz SLR	626 bhp at 6,500 rpm	3.7	208 / 332.8	3,898 lbs / 1,768 kg	183 in / 4,656 mm
Mitsubishi Lancer Evo VIII MR FQ·400	405 bhp at 6,400 rpm	3.5	175 / 280	3,086 lbs / 1,400 kg	177 in / 4,490 mm
Pagani Zonda S 7.3	555 bhp at 5,900 rpm	3.6	220 / 352	2,976 lbs / 1,350 kg	173 in / 4,395 mm
Porsche Carrera GT	612 bhp at 8,000 rpm	3.8	205 / 328	3,042 lbs / 1,380 kg	182 in / 4,613 mm
IVR Sagaris	406 bhp at 7,000-7,500 rpm	3.7	175 / 280	2,376 lbs / 1,078 kg	160 in / 4,057 mm
TVR Tuscan 2	350 bhp at 7,200 rpm	4.2	175 / 280	2,425 lbs / 1,100 kg	167 in / 4,235 mm
Bugatti Veyron	987 bhp at 6,000 rpm	3	252 / 403.2	4,299 lbs / 1,950 kg	172 in / 4,380 mm

Glossary

acceleration The change in velocity over time.

aerodynamic Describing the shape of an object and its ability to move with the least amount of air resistance.

BPH Brake horsepower, refers to the horsepower of an engine before the loss in horsepower of auxiliary components such as the gearbox.

cc (cubic centimeters) The volume measurement cubic centimeters.

chassis A frame that provides support for a structure.

displacement The volume of air and fuel a cyllinder can hold.

double wishbone A suspension system with two wishbone-shaped constructs.

fuel injection A system that forces pressurized fuel into an internal combustion engine.

handling An automobile's responsiveness to the driver.

maximum speed The top speed that a car can reach without wind resistance.

rack and pinion A type of steering system that has a pinion gear at the end of a steering shaft.

rpm Rotations per minute, or the rate at which a component within an engine spins.

six-speed An automobile that has six gear within its transmission.

suspension The system on a vehicle that cushions and protects it and the passenger from road vibration.

torque The turning force applied by the engine to the drivetrain of a vehicle.

transmission The mechanism in a car by which the engine's power is transmitted to the rear wheel.

turbocharge To add speed or energy to a car engine.

twin-turbo An engine that utilizes two turbochargers.

valvetrain In general, the components that operate the valves within the engine.

For More Information

Bugatti Automobiles S.A.S.
1, Château Saint Jean
Dorlisheim
67120 Molsheim
France
Web site: http://www.bugatti.com
Bugatti is a French manufacturer of some of the most high-end automobiles in the world.

duPont Registry
3051 Tech Drive
St. Petersburg, FL 33716
(888) 418-1126
Web site: http://www.dupontregistry.com
The duPont Registry is a publication devoted to the sale of some of the rarest "supercars" in the world.

Ferrari SpA
Via Abetone Inferiore n. 4
Italy
I-41053 Maranello (MO)
+39 0536 949111
Web site: http://ww.ferrari.com
Ferrari is among the best-known manufactuerers of super high-performance luxury vehicles.

Web Sites

Due to the changing nature of Internet links, Rosen Publishing has developed an online list of Web sites related to the subject of this book. This site is updated regularly. Please use this link to access the list:

http://www.rosenlinks.com/GEAR/Scars

For Further Reading

Adatto, Richard, Christina Japp, Julius Kruta, and Michael Furman. *The Art of Bugatti: Mullin Automotive Museum*. Philadelphia, PA: Coachbuilt, 2010.

Brümmer, Elmar, and Frank M. Orel. *Generation Porsche: An Album of Living History*. Kempen, Germany: TeNeues, 2009.

Carugati, Decio G. R. *Automobili Lamborghini*. Milan, Italy: Electa, 2009.

Codling, Stuart, and James Mann. *Form Follows Function: The Art of the Supercar*. Minneapolis, MN: Motor, 2011.

Graham, Ian. *Supercars*. London, England: QED, 2010.

Lamm, John. *Exotic Cars*. Minneapolis, MN: MBI Publishing, 2008.

Lamm, John, Larry Edsall, and Steve Sutcliffe. *365 Sports Cars You Must Drive*. Minneapolis, MN: MBI Publishing, 2011.

Lewin, Tony. *AZ of 21st Century Cars*. London, England: Merrell, 2011.

Mueller, Mike. *Motor City Muscle: The High-powered History of the American Muscle Car*. Minneapolis, MN: Motor, 2011.

Newhardt, David. *American Muscle Supercars: Ultimate Street Performance from Shelby, Baldwin-Motion, Mr. Norm, and Other Legendary Tuners*. Minneapolis, MN: MBI Publishing, 2008.

Newhardt, David, and Peter Harholdt. *Art of the Muscle Car*. Minneapolis, MN: MBI Publishing, 2009.

Phillips, Adam. *Supercars: Driving the Dream*. Sywell, England: Igloo, 2008.

Robson, Graham. *Inside the BMW Factories: Building the Ultimate Driving Machine*. Minneapolis, MN: MBI Publishing, 2008.

Tomalin, Peter, and David Lillywhite. *60 Years of Ferrari Supercars*. Wollaston, England: Dennis Publishing, 2007.

West, Ted. *American Road Warriors: Classic Muscle Cars*. New York, NY: Filipacchi Publishing, 2008.

Index